Learn to Speak and Write RUSSIAN

Vasuda Bhaskar

Lotus PRESS
4735/22, Prakash Deep Building,
Ansari Road, Daryaganj,
New Delhi - 110002

Lotus Press : Publishers & Distributors
Unit No. 220, 2nd Floor, 4735/22, Prakash Deep Building,
Ansari Road, Darya Ganj, New Delhi- 110002
Ph.: 41325510, 98118-38000
• E-mail : lotuspress1984@gmail.com
www.lotuspress.co.in

Learn to Speak and Write Russian

ISBN: 978-81-8382-293-0

Printed & Published by : **Lotus Press Publishers & Distributors,** New Delhi-02

Preface

This book is aimed at students, tourists, businessmen and anyone who is keen on learning colloquial Russian, rather than longer-term language learners. This book focuses on situations from everyday life. It comprises of a brief grammar of Russian. It has dialogues from everyday life, which have been translated and transliterated. The book comprises of 11 thematic chapters. Each chapter deals with grammar, vocabulary and dialogues. In addition to this, there are two glossaries at the end of the book for quick reference and also to enhance the readers vocabulary of Russian.

I am greatly indebted to Mr. A.J. Sehgal, for giving me the opportunity to write this book.

I would like to express my gratitude to my parents, without whose persistent encouragement and support I would have never been able to bring this book to completion. They have provided me plenty of food for thought on motivation.

As a teacher of Russian my challenge is always to help students to become more motivated to learn a foreign language, so that they have a clear purpose in learning a language, find a meaning in it, engage in it and finally become autonomous learners and users of the target language.

Vasuda Bhaskar

Contents

Contents

CHAPTER

1 Introduction

There are 33 letters in the Russian language; however there exist many more sounds as one and the same letter can indicate several sounds. Russian letters also have two different forms for capital and small letters both in writing as well as printing.

Letters		Name of the Letter	Sound	Similar English Sounds
Printed	Hand Written			
Аа	*Аа*	а आ	[а]	like **ar** in “**far**”
Бб	*Бб*	бэ बै	[б]	like **b** in “**b**ut”
Вв	*Вв*	вэ वै	[в]	like **v** in “**v**oice”
Гг	*Гг*	гэ गै	[г]	like **g** in “**g**et”
Дд	*Дд*	дэ दै	[д]	like **d** in “**d**ay”
Ее	*Ее*	е यै	[йэ]	like **ye** in “**ye**t”
Ёё	*Ёё*	ёе यौ	[йо]	like **yo** in “**yo**ur
Жж	*Жж*	жэ ज्झे	[ж]	like **s** in “plea**s**ure”
Зз	*Зз*	Зэ ज़े	[з]	like **z** in “**z**one”
Ии	*Ии*	И ई	[и]	like **ee** in “m**ee**t”
Йй	*Йй*	short и य	[й]	like **y** in “bo**y**”

Кк	*Кк*	Ка का	[к]	like **k** in "s**k**ate"
Лл	*Лл*	Эл एल	[л]	like **l** in "**l**ook"
Мм	*Мм*	Эм एम	[м]	like **m** in "**m**ay"
Нн	*Нн*	Эн एन	[н]	like **n** in "**n**ot"
Оо	*Оо*	О ओ	[о]	like **or** in "p**or**t"
Пп	*Пп*	Пэ पै	[п]	like **p** in "s**p**oon"
Рр	*Рр*	Эр एर	[р]	like **r** in "**r**ock"
Сс	*Сс*	Эс एस	[с]	like **s** in "**s**moke"
Тт	*Тт*	Тэ ते	[т]	like **t** in "**t**ie"
Уу	*Уу*	У ऊ	[у]	like **oo** in "m**oo**n"
Фф	*Фф*	Эф एफ़	[ф]	like **f** in "**f**oot"
Хх	*Хх*	Ха खा	[х]	like **ch** in the Scottish "lo**ch**"
Цц	*Цц*	Цэ त्से	[ц]	like **ts** in "boo**ts**"
Чч	*Чч*	Чэ चे	[ч]	like **ch** in "**ch**air"
Шш	*Шш*	Ша शा	[ш]	like **sh** in "**sh**ell"
Щщ	*Щщ*	Ща श्चा	[щ]	like **sh ch** in "Dani**shch**arter" (pronounced as one word)
Ъ	*ъ*	hard sign		
Ы	*ы*	इ	[ы]	like **i** in "w**i**nd"

Ь	ь	soft sign		
Ээ	Ээ	Э ऐ	[э]	like **e** in "bet"
Юю	Юю	Ю यू	[йу]	like **you** in "**you**th"
Яя	Яя	Я या	[йя]	like **yar** in "**yar**d"

Transliteration of Russian Letters into Latin

- А-a
- Б-b
- В-v
- Г-g
- Д-d
- Е-e, je
- ё-jo,'o
- Ж-zh
- З-z
- И-i
- й-j
- К-k
- Л-l
- М-m
- Н-n
- О-o
- П-p
- Р-r
- С-s
- Т-t
- У-u
- Ф-f
- Х-kh
- Ц-ts
- Ч-ch
- Ш-sh
- Щ-shh
- Ъ-j
- Ы-y
- Ь-'
- Э-e
- Ю-ju,'u
- Я- ja,'a

All sounds in the Russian language are subdivided into Vowels and Consonants. In the Russian language we find 6 vowel sounds (stressed) and 10 letters denoting vowel sounds.

Vowel Sounds and Letters

Sounds	Letters
а, о, у, ы, и, э	а, о, у, ы, и, э, я, ё, ю, е

The vowels form syllables: there are as many vowels in a word as syllables.

The Consonants

Table of the Hard Consonats	Table of the Soft Consonants
МА - МО - МУ - МЭ - МЫ	МЯ - МЁ - МЮ - МЕ - МИ
БА - БО - БУ - БЭ - БЫ	БЯ - БЁ - БЮ - БЕ - БИ
ПА - ПО - ПУ - ПЭ–ПЫ	ПЯ - ПЁ - ПЮ - ПЕ – ПИ
ВА - ВО - ВУ - ВЭ - ВЫ	ВЯ - ВЁ - ВЮ - ВЕ - ВИ
ФА - ФО - ФУ - ФЭ–ФЫ	ФЯ - ФЁ - ФЮ - ФЕ – ФИ
ДА - ДО - ДУ - ДЭ - ДЫ	ДЯ - ДЁ - ДЮ - ДЕ - ДИ
ТА - ТО - ТУ - ТЭ - ТЫ	ТЯ - ТЁ - ТЮ - ТЕ - ТИ
НА - НО - НУ - НЭ - НЫ	НЯ - НЁ - НЮ - НЕ - НИ
ЛА - ЛО - ЛУ - ЛЭ - ЛЫ	ЛЯ - ЛЁ - ЛЮ - ЛЕ - ЛИ
ЗА - ЗО - ЗУ - ЗЭ - ЗЫ	ЗЯ - ЗЁ - ЗЮ - ЗЕ - ЗИ
СА - СО - СУ - СЭ – СЫ	СЯ - СЁ - СЮ - СЕ – СИ
ЦА - ЦО - ЦУ-ЦЭ - ЦЫ ЦЕ – ЦИ	ЧА - ЧЁ - ЧУ - ЧЕ – ЧИ ЧО ЩА - ЩЁ - ЩУ - ЩЕ - ЩИ ЩО
РА - РО - РУ - РЭ - РЫ	РЯ - РЁ - РЮ - РЕ – РИ
ЖА - ЖО - ЖУ - ЖЕ - ЖИ ЖЁ	
ША - ШО - ШУ - ШЕ - ШИ ШЁ	

ГА - ГО - ГУ - -	- - - ГЕ – ГИ
КА - КО - КУ - -	- - - КЕ - КИ
ХА - ХО - ХУ - -	- - - ХЕ – ХИ

The consonants do not form syllables. Consonants are subdivided into voiceless-voiced; hard-soft.

Voiceless-voiced Consonants

Voiced	б в д з ж г - - - - м н р л й
Voiceless	п ф т с ш к щ ц ч

Voiceless and voiced consonants distinguish the meaning of words. For example: ба́р - па́р, ко́т – го́д, жа́р – ша́р.

Hard-soft Consonants

pairs: **hard** **soft**	 б п в ф с з т д м н л р к г х б’ п’ в’ ф’ с’ з’ т’ д’ м’ н’ л’ р’ к’ г’ х’
not in pairs: **always hard** **always soft**	 ж ш ц щ ч й

The consonants of group A are pronounced in a hard way if they are followed by letters а, о, у, э, ы and softly after letters я, е, ё, ю, и, ь:

бра́т / бра́т / ब्रात : бра́ть / брат’ / ब्रात्व

бы́ть / быт’ / बित्व : би́ть/ б’ит’ / बीत्व

но́с / но́с / नोस : нёс / н’ос / नियोस

лу́к / лу́к / लूक : лю́к / л’ук / लियूक

Hardness-softness of the consonants distinguishes the words meaning.

For example:

бра́т (brother)–бра́ть (to take),

व ज़ाल в за́л v zál (in the hall)– взя́л (to take) वज्याल,

बिल бы́л býl (was)- би́л (to beat-past tense) बील

The letters **ъ - ь** do not indicate sounds. Letter **ъ** is used to render hardness /softness/ of preceding consonants; **ь** - renders softness of preceding consonants.

Table of Combinations of the Consonants

ВБА - ВБО - ВБИ ФПА - ФПО - ФПИ ЗКА [СКА] - СКА

ВВА - ВВО - ВВИ ФФА - ФФО - ФФИ ВКА [ФКА] - ФКА

ВМА - ВМО - ВМИ ФМА - ФМО - ФМИ ВДА [ВДА] - ВТА- [ФТА]

ВНА - ВНО - ВНИ ФНА - ФНО - ФНИ ВГА [ВГА] - ВКА - [ФКА]

ВЛА - ВЛО - ВЛИ ФЛА - ФЛО - ФЛИ ВДА [ВДА] - ВТА- [ФТА]

ВРА - ВРО - ВРИ ФРА - ФРО - ФРИ СДА [ЗДА] - ЗТА- [СТА]

ВДА - ВДО - ВДИ ФТА - ФТО - ФТИ ЗЛО - СЛО

ВГА - ВГО - ВГИ ФКА - ФКО - ФКИ ЗМА - СМА

ВЗА - ВЗО - ВЗИ ФСА - ФСО - ФСИ ЗВА - СВА

ВЖА - ВЖО - ВЖИ ФША - ФШО - ФШИ ЗНА - СНА

РА - ТРА - ВТРА [ФТРА] - СТРА - ВСТРА [ФСТРА]

КТО - ГДА - ГДЕ

РУ - ДРУ - КДРУ [ГДРУ] - СДРУ [ЗДРУ]

ДА - ЖДА - ЖДУ БА - ЖБА

ЛА - КЛА - ГЛА - ЗЛА - СЛА - ВЛА - ТЛА - ДЛА

АРТ - ОРТ - УРТ - УКР - УПР - УГР

АБРЬ - БРЯ

МНО - МНЕ - ДНА - ДНЕ - ДНИ - ГНА - ГНИ

БЬЯ - ВЬЯ - ПЬЁ - ПЬЮ - ВЬЁ - ВЬЮ - ЛЬЁ - ЛЬЮ

ИСК - СКЛА - ОРСК - ПОЛЬСК - КУРСК

КВА - ДВА - ЗВА - ТВА - ЖВА - СВА - ШВА

Vowels in Russian can be stressed and unstressed. Stress is the pronunciation of one vowel in a word with a greater force accompanied by an increase in the length of the sound compared with others ones; such a vowel is called stressed. Stress is marked by / ′ / which is placed above the stressed vowel.

Russian words may consist of one, two, three and more syllables, one of which is stressed.

In Russian the stress does not fall on some definite syllable of a word, it is free: **ма́ма [máma]** (mum, mother); стака́н **[stakán]**. Stress can distinguish words and grammar forms: **замо́к [zamók] – за́мок [zámak]** (a padlock - a castle); **до́м [dóm]- дома́ [damá]** (house- houses).

The stress may also change the meaning of words:

до́ма (at home) - дома́ (houses)

स्तोइत сто́ит [stóit] (costs) – стои́т [stait] (is standing) स्तइत

In an unstressed position the vowels o and aare pronounced like a weak A resembling the Hindi अ or still weaker.

[O]	[A, अ]
до́м	дома
[A, आ]	**[A**, अ]
ма́ма	стака́н

In an unstressed position the vowel **E** is pronounced as **И [И]**

Сестра́ [Sestrá] सिस्त्रा

The vowel **Ё** is always stressed.

Reading the Consonants

The letters **б, в, д, ж, г** in the end of word, preceding the voiceless consonants, are pronounced as their voiceless pairs, like **п, ф, т, с, ш, к.** For example:

ра́з [рас] - once, дру́г [друк] - friend , клу́б [клуп] - club, кро́вь[кроф’] - blood, эта́ж [иташ] - floor, оши́бка [ΛшипкΛ] – mistake, завтра [зафтрΛ] **- tomorrow, ло́жка** [лошкΛ] - **spoon.**

The letters **п, ф, т, ш, к,** preceding voiced consonants, are pronounced as their voiced pairs, as letters **б, в, д з, ж, г.** For example:

футб’о́л [фудбол] - football, вокз’а́л [вΛгзал]- railway station, сд’е́лать [зд’элать] - to do, пр’о́сьба [проз’бΛ] - **request.**

Pronounciation of the Consonants Combinations

-сч	-[щ]	:	счита́ть [щитат’]
-зч	-[щ]	:	расска́зчик [рΛскащик]
-жч	-[щ]	:	мужчи́на [мущина]
-тьс	-[ц]	:	учи́ться [учицΛ]
-тс	-[ц]	:	де́тский [д’эцкий]
-дс	-[ц]	:	схо́дство [схоцтвΛ]
-дц	-[ц]	:	два́дцать [двацыт’]
-тч	-[ч]	:	лётчик [л’оччик]
-дч	-[ч]	:	перево́дчик [п’ир’ивоччик]
-сш	-[ч/]	:	вы́сший [вышший]
-зш	-[ш]	:	из шко́лы [ишшколы]
-стн	-[сн]	:	у́стно [уснΛ]
-здн	-[зн]	:	по́здно [познΛ]
-вств	-[ств]	:	здра́вствуй [здравствуй]

CHAPTER

2 Let's Get Acquainted

Здра́вствуйте!	Hello!
Zdrávstvujte!	ज़्द्रासतूविच्चे !
До́брое у́тро! (до обе́да)	Good Morning!
Dóbroe útro! (do obéda)	दोबरे उतरा (द अबयदा)
До́брый де́нь! (по́сле обе́да)	Good Afternoon
Dóbryj dén'! (pósle obéda)	दोबरी जेन (पोसले अबयदा)
До́брый ве́чер!	Good evening!
Dóbryj vécher!	दोबरी वेछर
Здра́вствуйте!	How do you do?
Zdrávstvujte!	ज़्द्रासतूविच्चे ?
Ка́к дела́?	How are you?
Kák delá?	काक जिला
Спаси́бо, о́чень хорошо́.	I am fine thank you.
Spasíbo, óchen' khoroshó.	सपासिबा औछिन खराशो
До свидания!	Good-bye!
Dosvidanija!	दसवीदानया !
Пока!	Bye!
Poka!	पका
Спокойной ночи!	Goodnight!
Spokojnoj nochi!	सपाकोइनी नोछी
До скорой встречи!	See you soon!
Do skoroj vstrechi!	द सकोरए व्सत्रेछी
До завтра!	See you tomorrow!
Do zavtra!	द जाफत्रा

До встречи!	See you later!
Do vstrechi!	द व्सत्रेछी
До свида́ния!	Good- Bye!
Dosvidanija!	दसवीदानया!
Спаси́бо!	Thank you!
Spasibo!	स्पासीबा
Пожа́луйста !	Welcome!
Pozhaluijsta!	पजालूसता
Извини́те!/ Извини́!	Excuse me! / I am sorry!
Izvinite! / Izvini!	इजविनिच्य/इजविनि!
Мо́жно?	May (I)?
Mozhno?	मोझना?
Кто́ Вы́?	Who are you?
Kto vy?	क्तो वि?

Personal Pronouns

я- мы́	I /we
ja- my	या – मि
ты́ – вы́	You /you
tý - vy	ति – वि
о́н, она́, оно́ - они́	He, she, it- they
ón, oná, onó - oní	ओन, अना, अनो, अनी

1.	Меня́ (его́, её, ва́с) зову́т….	My (his, her, your) name is…..
	Menjá (egó[evo], ejo[eyo], vás) zovút….	मिनया (इवो, इयो, वास) जावुत
2.	Ка́к ва́с (тебя́, его́, её) зову́т?	What is your (his,her) name?
	Kák vás (tebjá, egó[evo], ejo[eyo]) zovút?	काक वास (चिब्या, इवो, इयो) जावुत

3.	Мне́ (тебе́, ва́м, ему́, , е́й).....	I am (you are, he is, she is)…..
	Mné (tebé, vám, emú, , éj).....	मिनये (चिब्या, वाम, ईमू, येई)
4.	Го́д (-а), ле́т	Years
	Gód (-a), lét	गोद (आ), लेएत
5.	И́мя	Name
	Ímja	इमिया
6.	Фами́лия	Surname
	Famílija	फामिलिया

Note!

Friends and good acquaintances usually address each other with "Ты". Saying: **«бу́дем на́ "ты́"» búdem ná "tý"**, the person whom you have just met implies that he/she wants to get on closer terms with you. In the context of formal relations or when you address an older or unknown person you should use "вы". Even if you address ONE person — the verb after **ВЫ́** is used in the 2nd person **plural form**.

In Russian sentence, there is no verb in the present tense

Кто́ вы́? Who are you?

któ vý?

Я тури́ст. I am a tourist.

ja turíst.

The word пожа́луйста/ pozhalujsta/ can be used in many situations:

1.	As a reply to Спаси́бо.	(Thank you)
	Spasibo	
2.	As a reply to Извини́те	(Excuse me)
	Izvinite.	
3.	As an invitation: Входи́те!	(Come in)

	Vkhodite!	व्खजीचे
4.	As an offer: Хоти́те ча́й**?**	(Would you like some tea?);
	Khotite chaj?	खाचीचे चाय
5.	As a request: Да́йте чай	(Would you like some tea?);
	Dajte chaj?	दायचे चाय
6.	As an offer to take something: Возьми́те**.**	(Take (have) some).
	Voz'mite.	व्जमीच

DIALOGUE - 1

Дава́йте познако́мимся. Davájte poznakómimsja.	**Let's get acquainted** दवायचे पज़्नाकोमितस्या
Меня́ зову́т Прака́ш , а ва́с?	My name is Prakash. And yours?
Menjá zovút Prakásh , a vás?	मिनया जावुत प्राकाश, आ वास?
Суми́т.	Sumit.
Sumit	सुमित।
Ка́к ва́ша фами́лия?	What is your surname?
Kák vásha famílija?	काक वाशा फामिलिया
Мо́я фами́лия Шарма́.	My surname is Sharma.
Mojá famílija Sharmá.	मया फामिलिया शर्मा
Ка́к ва́с мо́жно называ́ть.	How may I call you?
Kák vás mózhno nazyvát'.	काक वास मोजना नजीवात्व?
Называ́йте меня́ про́сто Прака́ш.	Just call me Prakash.
Nazyvájte menjá prósto Prakásh.	नजीवाईचे मीनिया प्रोस्ता, प्रकाश
Бу́дем на́ "ты́"!	Let's be on a first-name basis with each other.

Búdem ná “tý”!	बुदीम ना ती
Да, коне́чно.	Yes, of course.
Da, konéchno.	द कानएशना
Отку́да Вы́ прие́хали?	Where have you come from?
Otkúda Vý priékhali?	अतकूदा वि प्रियखली
Из И́ндии.	From India.
Iz Índii.	इज इनजी
Вы́ учи́тесь и́ли рабо́таете?	Do you study or work?
Vý uchítes’ íli rabótaete?	वि उछीचैस इली रबोत्येचे
Я учу́сь в университе́те.	I study in the university.
Ja uchús’ v universitéte.	या उछूस व उनीवैरसीचेचे
Ско́лько ва́м ле́т?	How old are you?
Skól’ko vám lét?	स्कोलका वाम लियत
Мне́ 20 ле́т.	I am 20 years old.
Mné 20 lét.	मिनये दावदसेच लियत

DIALOGUE - 2

Дэвид :	Здра́вствуйте.
David:	Hello.
Вера Ивановна:	Здра́вствуйте. Извини́те, Вы́ тури́ст? Ка́к ва́с зову́т?
	(Kák vás zovút?)
Vera Ivanovna:	Hello. Excuse me, are you a tourist? What is your name?
Дэвид:	Меня́ зову́т Дэвид Браун. Я студе́нт и я америка́нец.

	(Ja amerikánets).	या आमेरिकानन्यत्स
David:	My name is David Brown. I am a student and I am an American.	
Вера Ивановна:	О́чень прия́тно	
	(Óchen' prijátno),	ओछिन प्रियात्ना
	Дэвид. А я- ги́д	
	(ja- gíd)	
	Меня́ зову́т Вера Ивановна.	
Vera Ivanovna:	Glad to meet you David. I am a tourist guide. My name is Vera Ivanovna.	

In formal situations Russians often use both the first and the patronymic when speaking to one another: **Мария Ивановна**. For informal situations, just first names are used: **Мари́на, Ма́ша**.

Most of the time in informal settings they use a shortened form of the first name: **Ма́ша**. Many Russian names have a variety of shortened forms.

Compare the English and Russian sentence constructions:

-Что́ э́то?	What is this?
Chtó jéto	श्तो एता
-Э́то Аме́рика.	This is/It is America.
Jéto Amérika	एता अमेरिका

In the Russian sentence, there is no verb in the present tense. Notice that Э́то Jéto can be translated in many ways:

1. It (is);
2. This (is)/ There (are);
3. That (is)/Those (are).

The Noun

The Nouns have Gender, Number, Declension, and also are

subdivided into animate beings or inanimate object categories. Each Noun belongs to one of the three Genders: (Masculine, Feminine, Neuter), it can be in the singular or plural form and always in the form of one of the six cases. In sentences Nouns have different functions.

Кто́ э́то?	Who is this?
Któ jéto?	क्तो एता
Что́ э́то?	What is this?
Chtó jéto?	श्तो एता ?
Э́то Фёдор.	This is Fedor.
Jéto Fjodor.	एता फियोदर
Э́то до́м	This is a house.
Jéto dóm.	एता दोम
Э́то студе́нт	This is a student.
Jéto student.	एता स्तूजियन्त
Э́то кни́га.	This is a book.
Jéto kníga.	एता क्निगा
Э́то де́душка.	This is grandfather.
Jéto dédushka.	एता जियेदुशका
Э́то сто́л	This is a table.
Jéto stól.	एता स्तोल
Э́то па́па.	This is papa.
Jéto pápa.	एता पापा
Э́то сту́л	This is a chair.
Jéto stúl.	एता स्तूल

The question Кто́?	The question Что́?
is asked about animate nouns (words denoting persons or animals)	is about inanimate nouns (words denoting objects)

Country Language		Кто́? **Who?**		
		О́н **He**	Она **She**́	Они́ **They**
Россия́ Russia	ру́сский Russian	ру́сский	ру́сская	ру́сские
И́ндия India	хи́нди Hindi	инди́ец	индиа́нка	инди́йцы
США USA	англи́йский English	америка́нец	америка́нка	америка́нцы
Великобрита́ния Great Britian	англи́йский English	англича́нин	англича́нка	англича́не
Герма́ния Germany	неме́цкий German	Не́мец	не́мка	не́мцы
Фра́нция France	францу́зский French	францу́з	францу́женка	францу́зы
Ига́лия Itlay	италья́нский Italian	италья́нец	италья́нка	италья́нцы
Испа́ния Spain	испа́нский Spanish	испа́нец	испа́нка	испа́нцы
По́льша Poland	по́льский Polish	Поля́к	по́лька	поля́ки
Кита́й China	кита́йский Chinese	кита́ец	китая́нка	кита́йцы
Япо́ния Japan	япо́нский Japanese	япо́нец	япо́нка	япо́нцы

Gender of Nouns

Each Noun belongs to one of the three Genders: *Masculine, Feminine, Neuter.*

In most cases the Gender of the Nouns has a formal meaning; therefore it can be distinguished by the last letter of word (with the exception of nouns which have the ending **ь**).

The Gender of the Nouns

Masculine	Ending	Feminine	Ending	Neuter	Ending
сто́л table	- -	-ко́мната room	-а	-окно́ window	-о
студе́нт student	- -	-студе́нтка student (*f.*)	-а	-мо́ре Sea	-е
музе́й museum	- -	-земля́ earth	-я		
геро́й hero	- -	-семья́ family	-я		
де́нь day	-ь	-две́рь door	-ь		
слова́рь dictionary	-ь	-но́вость news	-ь		

The following nouns belong to the Masculine Gender:

- nouns, ending in the consonant:

hard stem – *сто́л, студе́нт.*

soft stem - *музе́й, геро́й.*

The Feminine Gender incorporates:

- nouns, ending in -А:

hard stem - *ко́мната, студе́нтка.*

- nouns, ending in -Я:

soft stem *–земля́, семья́, аудито́рия* [*auditórij,* औदितोरिया] *auditorium.*

The following nouns belong to the Neuter Gender:

- nouns ending in -O:

hard stem *–окно́.*

- nouns ending in -E:

soft stem *-мо́ре, зда́ние (zdánie,* ज़दानिये*) building.*

Remember!

1. Words ending in -A↵ -Я↵ , denoting males, are related to the Masculine Gender *–ю́ноша* [*júnosha,* यूनशा] *youth, мужчи́на* [*muzhchína,* मूशीना] *man, дя́дя* [*djádja,* ज़याज़या] *uncle.*
2. All nouns ending in -МЯ belong to the Neuter Gender- *и́мя* [*ímja,* इमया] *name* , *пла́мя* [*plámja,* पलामिया] *flame, пле́мя* [*plémja,* पलेमिया] *tribe, вре́мя* [*vrémja,* पलेमियाव्रेमिया] *time, зна́мя* [*známja,* ज़नामिया] *banner, се́мя* [*semja,* सीमया] *seed.*

If a word has in the end -Ь, it can belong to the Masculine or the Feminine Genders.

The Gender of Nouns ending in –Ь

	Masculine Gender		Feminine Gender
1.			но́чь [noch', नोछ] night мы́шь [mýsh', मीश] mouse ро́жь [rózh', रोज्झ] rye
2.	слова́рь [*slovár',* स्लोवार] dictionary		
3.	учи́тель [uchítel', उछीचल] teacher		
4.	янва́рь	यनवार	
	сентябрь	सीनचायाबर	
	февра́ль	फेवराल	

	октябрь अकच्याबर	
	апре́ль अप्रैल	
	ноя́брь नयाबर	
	ию́нь ईयून	
	дека́брь जेकाबर	
	ию́ль ईयूल	
	де́нь day	го́рдость [go'rdost', गोरदस्त] pride
5.		ско́рость [skórost', सकोरस्त] speed
		жи́дкость [zhi'dkos', ज्झीदकस्त] liquid
		две́рь door
6.	ко́рень [kóryen', कोरेन] root	тетра́дь notebook
	ци́ркуль [tsi'rkool', सिरकूल] compass	

In some cases awareness of Rules helps to determine the Gender of the Nouns

1. If the Noun ends in hissing letters and in -Ь, this Noun relates to the Feminine Gender.

Masculine Gender	Feminine Gender
лу́ч [lúch, लूच] ray	но́чь [nóch', नोछ] night
каранда́ш [karandásh, करनदास] pencil	мы́шь [मीश]
но́ж [nózh, नोज्झ] knife	ро́жь [रोज्झ]

2, 3, 4. The Masculine Gender comprises:

Nouns with suffixes:

- АРЬ – *слова́рь.* स्लवार

- ТЕЛЬ - учи́тель, писа́тель [*pisátel,* उछीचल, पीसाचेल].

Nouns - the names of the months;

5. The Feminine gender incorporates Nouns ending in *suffix* -ОСТЬ-

- *жи́дкость, го́рдость;*

6. In other cases it is recommended to consult the dictionary.

The Plural of Nouns

Чьи́ это книги?	"Whose books are these?"
Ch'í jeto knigi?	छी एता क्नीगी
Мои́.	"Mine."
Moí	मई

In the plural masculine and feminine nouns take the ending – ы or –и, and neuter the ending –а or –я.

Gender	Singular	Plural	Ending
Masculine Feminine	апельси́н orange конфе́та candy	апельсин**ы** oranges конфе́т**ы** candies	-Ы
Masculine	музе́й musuem портфе́ль briefcase но́ж knife	музе́**и** musuems портфе́л**и** briefcases ножи́ knives	-И
Feminine	бу́лка bun кастрю́ля pan ды́ня melon две́рь door	бу́лк**и** buns кастрю́л**и** pans ды́н**и** melons двер**и́** doors	
Neuter	окно́ window по́ле field зда́ние building	о́кн**а** windows пол**я́** fields здани**я́** buildings	-А -Я

Nouns belonging to the Masculine and Feminine Genders with hard stem in the plural possess the ending **-Ы** -*столы́, ко́мнаты* [*stolý,* स्तली], [*kómnaty,* कोम्नती]

- *Nouns belonging to the Masculine and Feminine Genders with soft stem and those which stem ends in* **-И, have the ending И;** *-музéи, ножи́, лéкции (lecture)* [*muzéi*], [*nozhí*], [*léktsi,* लएकत्सी,]
- *Nouns which stem terminates in -К, Г, Х, Ч, Ж, Ш, Щ, have ending* **И**
- *мáльчики boys, рýчки pens, кни́ги books, орéхи nuts, лýчи rays, нóчи nights, плáщи, карандáши* [*mál'chiki,* मालछीकी,], [*rúchki,* रूचकी], [*knígi,* क्नीगी], [*orékhi,* आरेएखी], [*lúchi,* लूछी], [*nóchi,* नोछी], [*pláshhi,* प्लाशी], [*karandásh,* करनदाशी]
- *Nouns with the Neuter Gender and ending in* -Ohave the ending **-A**
- *óкна, пи́сьма letters;* ókna, pís'ma
  ओकना, पीसमा
- Nouns of the Neuter Gender and ending in -E have the ending **-Я**
- *моря́ seas, здáния buildings;* morjá, zdánija
  मरया, ज़दानिया

Special Cases of the Formation of the Plural of Nouns

Masculine nouns taking the ending -A or -Я in the plural	Masculine and neuter nouns taking the ending -ЬЯ in the plural
гóрод – городá city- cities	сы́н – сы́новья son-sons
górod - gorodá	sýn - sýnov'ja
गोरद — गरदा	सीन — सीनाविया
дóм - домá house - houses	брáт – брáтья brother - brothers
dóm - domá	brát - brát'ja
दोम — दोमा	ब्रात — ब्राचिया

но́мер – номера́ number - numbers	дру́г – дру́зья friend - friends
nómer - nomerá	drúg - drúz'ja
नोमेर — नमेरा	द्रूक — द्रूजिया
гла́з – глаза́ eye - eyes	сту́л – сту́лья chair - chairs
gláz - glazá	stúl - stúl'ja
ग्लाज़ — ग्लाज़ा	स्तूल — स्तूलिया
учи́тель – учи́теля teacher - teachers	де́рево – де́ревья tree - trees
uchítel' - uchítelja	dérevo - dérev'ja
उछीचेल — उछीचेलया	ज़ेरेवा — जैरेविया

Remember!

		Nouns used only in the Singular	Nouns used only in the Plural
	Material Substantive:		
1.	**(a)**	**Names of chemical elements:**	
		желе́зо [zhelézo, जिलेज़ा] iron	де́ти [déti, जेची] children
		ме́дь [méd', मेद] copper	роди́тели, [roditeli, राजजीलची] очки́ [ochkí, अछकी] spectacles
			но́жницы [nózhnity, नोज्झनित्सी] scissors
			брю́ки [brjúki, ब्रयूकी] trousers
	(b)	**Names of liquids:**	
		вода́ [vodá, वदा] water	
		бензи́н [benzín, बेनज़ीन] petrol	

	(c) Names of food products:	
	хле́б [khléb, ख्लेब] bread	
	са́хар [sákhar, साखर] sugar	
	Nouns generated from the adjectives and from the verbs:	
2.	мо́лодость [mólodost’, मोलदस्त] youth	вы́боры [vý́bory, विबरी] elections
	пе́ние [pénie, पेनिए] singing	перегово́ры [peregovóry, पेरेगावोरी] talks
3.	**Nouns with the meaning of generalization:**	
	молодёжь [molodjozh’, मलाजयोज] youth	су́тки [sútki, सूतकी] day
	оде́жда [odézhda, अजेज्झदा] clothes	кани́кулы [kaníkuly, कानीकूली] vacation
	ме́бель [mébel’, मेबिल] furniture	

CHAPTER

3 Where Do You Work/Study/Live?

The Prepositional case of Nouns and Adjectives

Nominative Что?	Prepositional Где?	Ending
сто́л	на столе́ on the table	
университе́т	в университе́т**е** in the university	
музе́й	в музе́**е** in the musuem	
евро́па	в Евро́п**е** in Europe	-е
семья́	в семь**е́** in the family	
по́ле	в по́л**е** in the field	
окно́	на окн**е́** on the window	
пло́щадь	на пло́щад**и** at the square	
аудито́рия	в аудито́ри**и** in the auditorium	
планета́рий	в планета́ри**и** in the planetarium	-и
зда́ние	в зда́ни**и** in the building	

DIALOGUE - 1

Ира- Здра́вствуй, Бэн!

Zdrávstvuj, Bjen!

जद्रासतूईवीचे !

Ira- Hello Ben!

Бен- Приве́т, Ира!

Privét, Ira!

प्रिवियत इरा

Ben- Hello Ira!

Ира - Ка́к дела́?

Kák delá?

काक जिला?

Ira - How are you?

Бен - Спаси́бо, хорошо́. А у тебя́?

Spasíbo, khoroshó. A u tebjá?

स्पासिबा, खरशो. आ यू तेब्या?

Ben - I am fine, thank you. How about you?

Ира- Норма́льно. Ты́ у́же учи́шься?

Normál'no. Tý úzhe uchísh'sja?

नरमालना, ती उजे उछीछस्या?

Ira- I am okay. Have you joined classes?

Бэн- Да, у́же на́чал учи́ться. А ты́?

Da, úzhe náchal uchít'sja. A tý?

या उजे नाछल उछीतस्या?

Ben-Yes I have already joined classes. What about you?

Ира- Я учу́сь и да́же рабо́таю.

Ja uchús' i dázhe rabótaju.

या उघूस ई दाजे राबोतयू।

Ira- I study and work.

Ира - Скажи́, а где́ ты́ рабо́таешь?

Skazhí, a gdé tý rabótaesh'?

सकाजी आ गीजे ती रबोतयश?

Ira - Tell me, where do you work?

Бэн - Я рабóтаю в “Интурúсте” перевóдчиком.

Ja rabótaju v “Inturíste” perevódchikom.

या राबोतयू व इनतूरिस्ते पेरेवोदछिकम।

Ben - I work in “Intourist” as a translator.

Вóт фотогрáфия. Э́то моя́ семья. Э́то мóй отéц. Óн инженéр.

Vót fotográfija. Jéto mojá sem’já. Jéto mój otéts. Ón inzhenér.

वोत फताग्राफिया, एता मया सीमया, एता मोई आचियतस। ओन इंनजिनियर।

Here are the photographs. This is my family. This is my father. He is an engineer.

Ира - Гдé óн рабóтает?

Gdé ón rabótaet?

गिजय ओन राबोतयत?

Ira - Where does he work?

Бэн - Óн рабóтает нá завóде. Вóт моя́ мáма. Онá врáч. Онá рабóтает в больнúце.

Ón rabótaet ná zavóde. Vót mojá máma. Oná vrách. Oná rabótaet v bol’nítse.

ओन राबोतयत ना जावोज्दे, वोत मया मामा, अना व्रराच अना राबोतयत व बलनितस्य

Ben -He works in a factory. This is my mother. She is a doctor. She works in hospital.

Ира - А э́то ктó?

A jéto któ?

आ एता क्तो?

Ira-And who is this?

Бэн-Э́то мо́й бра́т.

Jéto mój brát.

एता मोई ब्रात।

Ben-This is my brother.

Ира-Кто́ о́н?

Któ ón?

क्तो ओन?

Ira-What is he?

Бэн - О́н студе́нт. Учи́тся в институ́те. А моя́ сестра́ рабо́тает в ба́нке. Во́т она́. А э́то де́душка и ба́бушка.

Ón studént. Uchítsja v institúte. A mojá sestrá rabótaet v bánke. Vót oná. A jéto dédushka i bábushka.

ओन सतूजियन्त उछीसया व इनसचीतूचय आ मया सिस्त्रा रबोतयत व बांके वोत अना आ एता जियदूसका ई बाबुराका।

Ben - He is a student. He studies in the institute. And my sister works in a bank. Here she is. And this is my grandfather and grandmother.

Ира - Ва́ша ба́бушка?

Vásha bábushka?

वाशा बाबुशका?

Ira - Your grandmother?

А э́то кто́?

A jéto któ?

आ एता क्तो?

And who is this?

Бэн - Э́то моя́ подру́га. Она́ актри́са.
Jéto mojá podrúga. Oná aktrísa.
एता मया पदरूगा अना अकत्रिसा।
Ben - This is my friend (female friend). She is an actress.

Ира - А где́ она́ рабо́тает?
A gdé oná rabótaet?
आ गीजय अना रबोतयत?
Ira - And where does she work?

Бэн - В теа́тре.
V teátre.
व त्यात्रे।
Ben - In the theatre.

А вы́ где́ рабо́таете?
A vý gdé rabótaete?
आ वि गिजे रबोत्यचे?
And where do you work?

Ира - Я рабо́таю в шко́ле. Я учи́тель (ница).
Ja rabótaju v shkóle. Ja uchítel' (uchítel'nitsa).
या राबोतयू व शकोले या उछीचल।
Ira - I work in a school. I am a teacher.

DIALOGUE - 2

Где́ вы́ живёте?
Gdé vý zhivjote?
गिजे वी जिवयोचे?
Where do you live?

Вы́ живёте в Москве́?

Vý zhivjote v Moskvé?

वि जिवु व म्सकव्य?

You live in Moscow?

Я живу́ в Де́ли. А вы́?

Ja zhívu v Déli. A vý?

या जिवू व दैली। आ वि?

I live in Delhi. And you?

Не́т, я жи́ву в Петербу́рге, а мо́й бра́т живёт в Москве́.

Nét, ja zhívu v Peterbúrge, a mój brát zhivjot v Moskvé

नियत या जीवू व पितेरबूरगे। आ, मोई ब्रात जिवयोत व मसक्व्य।

No, I live in Petersburg, and my brother lives in Moscow.

Мы́ живём в Канпу́ре.

Mý zhivjom v Kanpúre.

आ, मी जिवयोम व कानपुरे।

We live in Kanpur.

DIALOGUE - 3

То́м где́ ты́ бы́л у́тром?

Tóm gdé tý býl útrom?

तोम गिजे ति बिल ऊतरम?

Tom where were you in the morning?

Дома́. Смотре́л телеви́зор.

Domá. Smotrél televízor.

दोमा सम्त्रेल चेलेविजर।

At home. I was watching television.

Declension System

In the Russian language the nouns change depending on what function they play in sentence. Это Бори́с и Ни́на. Я давно знаю Ни́ну и Бори́са.

These different forms are called the case forms and the endings - the case endings. The case endings indicate at the same time the gender, the number and the case. There are 6 cases in the Russian language. Each case has its specific questions and every case form has variety of endings.

Nominative	Именительный	(И)	Кто́?, Что́?
Genitive	Родительный	(Р)	Кого́?, Чего́?
Dative	Дательный	(Д)	Кому́?, Чему́?
Accusative	Винительный	(В)	Кого́?, Чего́?
Instrumental	Творительный	(Т)	Ке́м?, Че́м?
Prepositional	Предложный	(П)	(о) Ко́м?, (о) Че́м?

The Nominative case is always used without preposition. Prepositional case is always used with preposition. The Genitive, Dative, Accusative and Instrumental cases are used without prepositions and with prepositions, which are always placed before nouns. The form of the Noun determines the form of adjectives, pronouns, numerals and participles agreed with this Noun.

The nominative case in the singular - is the starting form, on basis of which you can derive all the other forms of nouns. All the nouns in the dictionaries are given in the nominative case. Nominative case is always applied without prepositions.

The Russian, possessive pronouns change forms according to gender and number....

мо́й-*m*., моя́- *f*., моё- *n*., мои́- *pl*.

mój, mojá, mojo, moí

मोई, मया, मयो, मई

Personal and Possessive Pronouns

Personal pronouns	Possessive pronouns Singular			
я I	**Masculine**	**Feminine**	**Neuter**	
ты́ You о́н He она́ She оно́ It	**Че́й?** **Whose?** **chéj?**	**Чья́?** **Whose?** **ch'já?**	**Чьё?** **Whose?** **ch'jo?**	
	мо́й **mój** дом тво́й **tvój**	моя́ **mojá** квартира твоя́ **tvojá**	моё **mojo** окно твоё **tvojo**	My (mine) Your(s)
мы́ We вы́ You	его́, её (for all the genders and numbers) **egó, ejo**			His Her(s) Its
они́ They	на́ш **násh** дом ва́ш **vásh**	на́ша **násha** квартира ва́ша **vásha**	на́ше **náshe** окно ва́ше **váshe**	Our(s) Your(s)
	их **íkh** (for all the genders and numbers)			Their(s)

Adverbs of Place

-Где́ ва́ш до́м? **Gdé vásh dóm?**	"Where is your house?" गिज वाश दोम?
-На́ш до́м спра́ва. **Násh dóm správa**	"Our house is on the right." नाश दोम स्प्रावा

To convey location, the adverbs зде́сь **zdés'** (जेस) "here" (ту́т **tút** (तूत) "here"), та́м **tám** (ताम्) "there", спра́ва **správa** (स्प्रावा) "on the right", сле́ва **sléva** (स्लेवा) "on the left", ря́дом **rjádom** (रियादम) "beside", посереди́не **poseredíne** (पर्सिजिन्ने) "in the middle" and напро́тив **naprótiv** (नाप्रोचिव) "opposite" are used in Russian.

DIALOGUE - 4

Мари́я - Извини́те, где́ институ́т?

Maríja - Izviníte, gdé institút?

मरिया – इजविनीचे, गिजे, इनसचीतूत?

Maria – Excuse me, where is the institute?

Прохо́жий - Институ́т и́ли университе́т?

Prokhózhij - Institút íli universitét?

प्राखोजी – इनसचीतूत ईली ऊनीवेरसीचेयत?

Passerby – Institute or the University?

Мари́я - Институ́т.

Maríja - Institút.

मरिया – इनसचीतूत।

Maria – Institute.

Прохо́жий - Институ́т та́м спра́ва. Э́то далеко́. А университе́т ту́т, сле́ва.

Prokhózhij - Institút tám správa. Jéto dalekó. A universitét tút, sléva.

प्राखोजी – इनसचीतूत ताम स्प्रावा, एता दलीको आ, उनीवेरसिचेत तूत, स्लेवा।

Passerby: Institute is on the right. It is far. And the university is here, on the left.

Дэвид - Спаси́бо. А та́м рестора́н?

Djevid - spasíbo. A tám restorán?

डेविड – स्पसीबा, आ ताम, रस्तारान?

David – Thank you. And the restaurant is there?

Прохо́жий – Не́т, та́м не́ рестора́н, та́м магази́н.А рестора́н ря́дом.

Prokhózhij – Nét, tám né restorán, tám magazín. A restorán rjádom.

नीयत ताम नी रेसत्रारान, ताम मगाज़ीन आ रेसतारान रियादम।

Passerby – No, there is no restaurant, there is a shop there. The restaurant is nearby.

Дэвид - А что́ зде́сь?

Djevid - A chtó zdés'?

डेविड – आ श्तो जेस?

David - And what is here?

Прохо́жий - Зде́сь кафе́.

Prokhózhij - Zdés' kafé.

जेस काफे।

Passerby - A café.

Дэвид - Извини́те, а где́ метро́?

Djevid - Izviníte, a gdé metró?

डेविड – इजवनीचे आ गीजे मेतरो?

David - Excuse me, where is the metro?

Прохо́жий - Во́н та́м, напро́тив.

Prokhózhij - Vón tám, naprótiv.

वोन ताम नाप्रोचिव।

Passerby - Over there, right opposite.

Дэвид – Спаси́бо.

Djevid - Spasíbo

डेविड – स्पसीबा।

David - Thank you.

Прохо́жий – Пожа́луйста.

Prokhózhij - Pozhálujsta

पजालूस्ता।

Passerby - Welcome.

The Verb

The Present Tense	The 1st And 2nd Verb Conjugations
Что́ ты́ де́лаешь?	"What are you doing?"
Chtó tý délaesh'?	शतो ती जेलयश
Чита́ю журна́л.	"I am reading a journal."
Chitáju zhurnál.	छितायु ज्झूरनाल

The present tense of the Russian verb corresponds to the English Present Indefinite, Present Continuous and Present Perfect. In the present tense verbs conjugate (change for person and number). Each person has own ending.

1st Conjugation Verbs

Infinitive	**Чита́ть Chitát' To Read**	**Писа́ть с/ш Pisát' To Write**	**Endings**
Singular number	я чита́**ю** ja chitáju I read/ I am reading ты чита́**ешь** ty chitáesh' You read/ You are reading он (а) чита́**ет** on (a) chitáet He/She reads/ is reading	я пишу́ ja pishú I write/ I am writing ты пи́ш**ешь** ty pishésh' You write/ You are writing он (а) пиш**е́т** on (a) pishét He/She writes/ is writing	-Ю -ЕШЬ -ЕТ
Plural number	мы чита́**ем** my chitáem We read/ We are reading вы чита**е́те** vy chitaéte You read/ You are reading они чита́**ют** oni chitájut They read/ They are reading	мы пиш**е́м** my pishém We write/ We are writing вы пиш**е́те** vy pishéte You write/ You are writing они пиш**у́т** oni pishút They write/ They are writing	-ЕМ -ЕТЕ -ЮТ, -УТ
Imperative Singular Number Plural Number	чита́**й**! chitáj! Read! чита́й**те**! chitájte!	пиш**и́**! pishí! Write! пиш**и́те**! pishíte!	-Й, -АТ -ТЕ

2nd Conjugation Verbs

Infinitive	**Говори́ть To Speak Govorít'**	**Учи́ть To Study Uchít'**	**Endings**
Singular number	я говор**ю́** ja govorjú I speak/ I am speaking ты говор**и́шь** ty govorísh' You speak/ You are speaking он (а) говор**и́т** on (a) govorít He/She speaks/ is speaking	я уч**у́** ja uchú I study/ I am studying ты уч**и́шь** ty uchísh' You study/ You are studying он (а) уч**и́т** on (a) uchít He/She studies/ is studying	-Ю, -У -ИШЬ -ИТ
Plural number	мы говор**и́м** my govorím We speak/ We are speaking вы говор**и́те** vy govoríte You speak/ You are speaking они говор**я́т** oni govorját They speak/ They are speaking	мы уч**и́м** my uchím We study/ We are studying вы уч**и́те** vy uchíte You study/ You are studying они уч**а́т** oni uchát They study/ They are studying	-ИМ -ИТЕ -ЯТ, -АТ
Imperative Singular Number Plural Number	говор**и́**! govorí! Speak! говор**и́те**! govoríte!	уч**и́**! uchí! Study! уч**и́те**! Uchíte	-И -ТЕ

1. Endings in the 1st person, singular of the 1st and 2nd conjugations coincide.
2. Ending –И in the Imperative- after the consonants.
3. Ending –АТ, -УТ —after the consonants Ж, Ш, Щ, Ч: слышат, пишут.
4. In the second person, singular Ш is always followed by Ь: чита́ешь, говори́шь.

The verb conjugation of люби́ть [ljubít', लियूबित] to love, гото́вить [gotóvit', गतोविच] to prepare, **с**пать [spat', स्पाच] to sleep; has specific features.

ЛЮБИ́ТЬ – **To love**

я люблю́ подарки. ja ljubljú podarki. या ल्यूबलू पदारकी। I love gifts.	**мы люби́м подарки.** my ljubím podarki. मी ल्यूबिम पदारकी। We love gifts.
ты люби́шь подарки. ty ljubísh' podarki. ती ल्यूबिश पदारकी। You love gifts.	**вы люби́те подарки.** vy ljubíte podarki. वी ल्यूबिचे पदारकी। You love gifts.
он/она люби́т подарки. on/ona ljubít podarki. ओन/अना ल्यूबित पदारकी। He/She loves gifts.	**они любя́т подарки.** oni ljubját podarki. अनी ल्यूब्यात पदारकी। They love gifts.

The Past Tense of the Verb

The past tense is formed by adding the suffix **-л** and the ending –а (for feminine), the ending **-о** (for neuter) and **-и** (for plural).

Чита́-ть (To read) Chitát' – чита́-л (Read)

чита́-ла

чита́-ло

чита́-ли

я чита́л
ja chitál
या छिताल
I read

мы́ чита́ли
mý chitáli
मी छिताली
We read

ты́ чита́л
tý chitál
ती छिताला
You read

вы́ чита́ли
vý chitáli
वी छिताली
You read

о́н чита́л, она́ чита́ла
они́ чита́ли oní chitáli
ón chitál, oná chitála
ओन छिताल, अना छिताला, अनो छितालो
He reads, She reads.
They read.

The Verb [БЫ́ТЬ (To Be)]

Present		Past	
о́н она́ они́	в музе́е	о́н бы́л ón býl ओन बिल она́ бы́ла oná býla अना बिला они́ бы́ли oní býli अनी बिली	**Went** в музе́е
Сего́дня четве́рг. Segódnja chetvérg. Today is Thursday.		Вчера бы́л вто́рник. Vchera býl vtornik. व्चीरा बिल फ्तोरनिक। Yesterday wasTuesday.	

У на́с уро́к. U nás urók. We have a class.	У на́с бы́л уро́к. U nás býl urók. उ नास बिल उरोक। We had a class.
У ва́с экза́мен. U vás jekzámen. You have an exam.	У ва́с бы́л экза́мен. U vás býl jekzámen. उ वास बिल इकजामिन। You had an exam.

The verb **е́сть est'** is the invariable present tense form of the verb **бы́ть být'**. The verb **бы́ть** is used in the past tense and future tense and not in the present tense.

The Future Tense of the Verb

Inf. Пе́ть pét'

я бу́ду пе́ть
ja búdu pét'
या बुदू पेच
ты́ бу́дешь пе́ть
tý búdesh' pét'
ती बुदीश पेच
он (а) бу́дет пе́ть
on (a) búdet pét'
ओन बुदीत पेच
мы́ бу́дем пе́ть
mý búdem pét'
मी बुजीम पेच
вы́ бу́дете пе́ть
vý búdete pét'
वी बुजीचे पेच

они́ бу́дут пе́ть
oní búdut pét'
अनी बुदुत पेच

The verb **бы́ть** in the future tense conveys the meaning of **Will/Shall.**

The Verb (БЫТЬ)

Present		Future	
о́н	в университе́те is in the university	о́н бу́дет he will/shall	в университе́те be in the university
она́		она́ бу́дет she will/shall	
они́		они́ бу́дут they will/shall	
Сего́дня четве́рг. Today is Thursday.		За́втра бу́дет пя́тница. Závtra búdet pjátnitsa. Tomorrow is Friday.	
У на́с уро́к. We have a class.		У на́с бу́дет уро́к. U nás búdet urók. We will have a class.	
У ва́с экза́мен. You have an exam.		У ва́с бу́дет экза́мен. U vás búdet jekzámen. You will have an exam.	

The Verb –is a changeable part of speech which has its own endings.

The verb specifies:

an action:

Студе́нт чита́ет.

studént chitáet.

स्तूजियन्त छितायत

The student reads/ The student is reading.

or a state, condition:

Ма́льчик боле́ет.
mál'chik boléet.

मालछिक बालेयत

The boy is ill.

The main function of Verb in a sentence is to serve as the predicate.

(A) Verb Aspects

Verbs may have perfective and imperfective aspects.

Meaning of the Verb Aspects

Meanings of the Imperfective Verb Aspect

1.	**Name of action**	Ты́ чита́л стихи́ Пу́шкина? tý chitál stikhí púshkina? ती छिताल स्तिखी पुशकिना ? Did you read Pushkin's poem?
		Чита́л. chitál. छिताल। I did.
		Я хорошо́ пла́ваю. ja khoroshó plávaju. या खराशो प्लावयू। I swim well.

<table>
<tr><td rowspan="2">2.</td><td rowspan="2">Process of action</td><td>Ты́ до́лго писа́л пи́сьма?
tý dólgo pisál pís'ma?
ती दोलगा पिसाल पिसमा ?
Did you write letters for a long time?</td></tr>
<tr><td>Я пи́сал пи́сьма ве́сь ве́чер.
ja písal pís'ma vés' vécher.
या पिसाल पिसमा वेस वेछर।
I wrote letters the whole evening.</td></tr>
<tr><td>3.</td><td>Repeated action</td><td>Я ча́сто пи́шу пи́сьма дру́гу.
ja chásto píshu pís'ma drúgu.
या छास्ता पिशू पिसमा द्रूगू।
I often write letters to a friend.</td></tr>
<tr><td rowspan="2">4.</td><td rowspan="2">Simultaneous actions (in simple and complex sentence)</td><td>Я писа́л пи́сьма и слу́шал му́зыку.
ja pisál pís'ma i slúshal múzyku.
या पिसाल पिसमा इ स्लूशल मूज़िकु।
I wrote letters and listened to the music.</td></tr>
<tr><td>Когда́ я пи́сал пи́сьмо, мо́й дру́г чита́л га́зету.
kogdá ja písal pís'mo, mój drúg chitál gázetu.
कगदा या पिसाल पिसमो, मोइ द्रुक छिताल गाज़्येतू।
When I was writing the letter, my friend was reading the newspaper.</td></tr>
</table>

Meanings of Perfective Aspect Verbs

1.	**Effectiveness (completeness)**	Я у́же прочита́л эту́ кни́гу, ты́ мо́жешь взя́ть её. ja úzhe prochitál jetú knígu, tý mózhesh' vzját' ejo. या उज्झे प्रछिताल ऐतु क्निगु, ती मोज्झिश व्ज़याच। I have already ready this book, you can take it.
2.	**Momentary aspect of action**	Одна́жды я встре́тил своего́ дру́га. odnázhdy ja vstrétil svoegó shkól'nogo drúga. अदनीज्झदी या व्सस्त्रेचिल स्वयेवो श्कोलनवा द्रुगा। Once I met my friend.
3.	**Consequence of completed actions. (in simple and complex sentences)**	Я купи́л конве́рт и написа́л а́дрес. ja kupíl konvért i napisál ádres. या कुपील कनव्यर्त इ नापिसाल आद्रेस। I bought an envelope and wrote the address.
		Когда́ я написа́л пи́сьмо, я пошёл на́ по́чту. kogdá ja napisál pís'mo, ja poshjol ná póchtu. कगदा या नापिसाल पिस्मो, या पश्योल ना पोछ्तु। When I wrote the letter, I went to the post office.

Important!

Imperfective Aspect	Perfective Aspect
Two (or more) parallel actions:	**Single action (Perfective aspect) against a background of the other (Imperfective aspect):**
Вчера́ я чита́л те́кст и переводи́л но́вые слова́. Vcherá ja chitál tékst i perevodíl nóvye slová. व्छेरा या छिताल चेक्स्त इ पेरेवाजील नोवे स्लवा। Yesterday I read a text and translated new words.	Когда́ я отдыха́л, пришёл мо́й дру́г. Kogdá ja otdykhál, prishjol mój drúg. कगदा या अतदीखाल, प्रिश्योल मोइ द्रुक। When I was resting, my friend came.
Когда́ я отдыха́л, мо́й дру́г слуша́л му́зыку. Kogdá ja otdykhál, mój drúg slushál múzyku. कगदा या अतदिखाल, मोइ द्रुक स्लूशल मूजिकु। When I was resting, my friend was listening to the music.	

Forms for Expression of the Start of Action (State)

Verb НАЧААТЬ	Verbs of Motion Prefix ПО-	Some Verbs Prefix ЗА-
Я прочита́л пи́сьмо и на́чал писа́ть отве́т. Ja prochitál pís'mo i náchal pisát' otvét. या प्रछिताल पिस्मो इ नाछल पिसाच अतव्येत। I read the letter and started writing the reply.	Я написа́л пи́сьмо и пошёл на́ по́чту. Ja napisál pís'mo i poshjol ná póchtu. या नपिसाल पिस्मो इ पश्योल ना पोछ्तु। I wrote the letter and went to the post office.	Я услы́шал весёлый расска́з и засмея́лся. Ja uslýshal vesjolyj rasskáz i zasmejálsja. या उस्लीशल रस्काज़ इ ज़ास्मीयालस्या। I heard the funny story and laughed.
Мы́ переведём статьи́, а пото́м начнём переводи́ть стихи́. Mý perevedjom stat'í, a potóm nachnjom perevodít' stikhí. मी पेरेविज्योम स्ताची, आ पतोम नछन्योम पेरेवाजिछ स्तिखी। We will translate the article, and then we will start translating the poem.	Я око́нчу университе́т и пое́ду домо́й Ja okónchu universitét i poédu domój. या अकोन्छू उनीवेरसीच्येत इ पयेदु दामोय। I will complete the university and go home.	

Нача́ть + Infinitive of Imperfective aspect (not the verbs of motion)	По + verbs of motion	ЗА + смея́ться молча́ть пе́ть говори́ть пла́кать (some verbs)

(b) Verb Tenses

Verb has three tenses: present, past and future. The future tense has two forms:

simple - for perfective aspect verbs:

- *За́втра я прочита́ю стихи́;*

Závtra ja prochitáju stikhí.

जाफतरा या प्रछिताय़ू स्तीखी।

Tomorrow I will read the poem.

and complex - for imperfective aspect verbs:

- *За́втра я бу́ду чита́ть стихи́.*

Závtra ja búdu chitát' stikhí.

जाफतरा या बूदू छिताच स्तीखी।

Tomorrow I wil! read the poem.

Meaning of the Verb Tenses

Past		Present	Future
Action in the past, before the moment of speech:		**Action at the moment of speech:**	**Action after the moment of speech:**
Что́ ты́ де́лал вчера́? -Ходи́л в кино́. Chtó ty dyélal vchyerá?khodíl v kinó. श्तो ती जेलल व्छेरा? खजील व किनो। *What did you do yesterday? I went to the cinema.*	1.	*Что́ ты́ де́лаешь сейча́с?* Chtó tý délaesh' sejchás? श्तो ती जेलयेश सिछास? *What are you doing now?*	*Что́ ты́ бу́дешь де́лать за́втра?* Chtó tý búdesh' délat' závtra? श्तो ती बुजेश जेलच जाफत्रा? *What will you do tomorrow?*
		Пи́шу пи́сьмо. Píshu pís'mo. पिशु पिसमो। *I am writing a letter.*	*За́втра я бу́ду отдыха́ть.* Závtra ja búdu otdykhát'. जाफत्रा या बुदु अतदीखाच। *Tomorrow I will rest.*
	2.	**Action which started before and is continuing at the present moment:**	
		Я жи́ву в Москве́ 3 го́да. Ja zhívu v Moskvé 3 góda. या ज्झिवु व मस्कवे त्रि गोदा। *I am living in Moscow for three years.*	*Что́ ты́ сдела́ешь за́втра?* Chtó tý sdeláesh' závtra? श्तो ती जेलयेश जाफत्रा? *What are you doing tomorrow?*

		Permanent action:	
	3.	*Пти́цы лета́ют.* Ptítsy letájut. प्चीत्सी लेतायुत। *The birds are flying.*	*Напи́шу пи́сьмо́, пото́м прочита́ю кни́гу, и ты́ смо́жешь взять её.* Napíshu pis'mó, potóm prochitáju knígu, i tý smózhesh' vzjat' ejo. नपिशु पिस्मो, पतोम प्रछितायु क्नीगु, इ ती स्मोज्झिश व्ज्याच इयो। *I will write a letter,then I shall read a book and you can take it then.*

Tenses of Imperfective and Perfective Verbs

Verbs aspect	Past tense	Present Tense	Future Tense
Imperfective aspect	*Я писа́л письмо́.* Ja pisál pis'mó. या पिसाल पिस्मो। I wrote a letter.	*Я пи́шу письмо́.* Ja píshu pis'mó. या पिशू पिस्मो। I am writing a letter.	*Я бу́ду писа́ть письмо́.* Ja búdu pisát' pis'mó. या बुदू पिसाच पिस्मो। I will write a letter.

Perfective aspect	*Я написал письмо.* Ja napisál pis'mó. या नपिसाल पिस्मो। I wrote a letter.	---------------------	*Я напишу письмо.* Ja napíshu pis'mó. या नपिशू पिस्मो। I will write a letter.
	Verbs of imperfective and perfective aspects has one form in the past tense	Verbs of the perfective aspect do not have the form of the present tense	Verbs of imperfective aspect have complex form in the future tense and verbs of perfective aspect have the form in the future simple tense.

FORMS OF VERB

Verb Infinitive

This is unchangeable, (basic) form of verb.

Suffixes of the Infinitive

Majority of verbs	Some verbs	Some words
чита́**ть** звони́**ть** To ring	ид**ти́** To go	мо́**чь** may/can
ТЬ смея́**ть**ся To laugh	нес**ти́** To carry	помо́**чь** To help
	ТИ спас**ти́**сь To escape	ЧЬ бере́**чь**ся To beware

Some verbs take the particle -СЯ:

after consonants	after vowels
СЯ встреча́ться To meet	СЬ спасти́сь нести́сь To rush along
учи́ться To study	

The use of Infinitive in the Imperfective and Perfective Aspects.

1. After verbs		
хоте́ть to want	Я хочу́ игра́ть. Ja Khochú igrát'. या खचू इग्राच ! I want to play.	Я хочу́ купи́ть га́зету. Ja Khochú kupít' gázetu. या खचू कुपीच गाज़्येतु। I want to buy a newspaper.
мо́чь can/may	Я уме́ю рисова́ть. Ja uméju risovát'. या उमेयू रिसावाच। I can draw.	Я могу́ помо́чь ва́м. Ja mogú pomóch' vám. या मगू पमोछ वाम। I can help you.

сове́товать to advice	Я сове́тую бо́льше чита́ть по-ру́сски. Ja sovétuju ból'she chitát' po-rússki. या सव्येतूयू बोल्शे छिताच पारूस्की। I advice you to read more Russian.	Я сове́тую ва́м пойти́ в те́атр. Ja sovétuju vám pojtí v téatr. या सव्येतूयू वाम पइची व च्यातर। I advice you to go to the theatre.
проси́ть to forgive	Я прошу́ ва́с писа́ть пи́сьма. Ja proshú vás pisát' pís'ma. या प्रशू वास पिसाच पिस्मा। I request you to write letters.	Я прошу́ ва́с позвони́ть мне́ за́втра. Ja proshú vás pozvonít' mné závtra. या प्रशू वास पज़्वानीच मिन्ये ज़ाफत्रा। I request you to call me up tomorrow.
2. After verbs of motion:		
идти́ пойти́ прийти́ поехать и.т.д.	Мы́ прие́хали учи́ться. Mý priékhali uchít'sja. मी प्रीयेखली उछीतस्या। We came to study.	
	Я пойду́ в магази́н купи́ть тетра́ди. Ja pojdú v magazín kupít' tetrádi. या पइदू व मगाज़ीन कुपीच चितराजी। I shall go to the shop to buy notebooks.	

3. With words:		
на́до ну́жно мо́жно	Ва́м ну́жно мно́го занима́ться. Vám núzhno mnógo zanimát'sja. वाम नूज्झना म्नोगा ज़नीमात्स्या। You must study a lot.	Мо́жно войти́? Mózhno vojtí? मोज्झना वइची? May I come in?
	Ва́м мо́жно выходи́ть на у́лицу. Vám mózhno vykhodít' na úlitsu. वाम मोज्झना विखाजीच ना उलित्सू। You may go out.	Ва́м мо́жно пое́хать отдохну́ть. Vám mózhno poékhat' otdokhnút'. वाम मोज्झना पयेखच अतदखनूछ। You can go and rest.
4. With adverbs terminating in –O		
прия́тно тру́дно легко́ интере́сно	Мне́ прия́тно разгова́ривать с ва́ми. Mné prijátno razgovárivat' s vámi. मिन्ये प्रीयात्ना रज़गवारीवछ स्वामी। It is a pleasure to talk to you.	Мне́ прия́тно познако́миться с ва́ми. Mné prijátno poznakómit'sja s vámi. मिन्ये प्रियात्ना पज़्नाकोमित्स्या स्वामी। It is a pleasure meeting you.

	Мне́ тру́дно писа́ть. Mné trúdno pisát'. मीन्ये त्रूना पिसाच। It is difficult for me to write.	Мне́ бу́дет тру́дно сда́ть экза́мен. Mné búdet trúdno sdát' jekzámen. मिन्ये बूजित त्रूना ज़्दाच इक्ज़ामिन। It will be difficult for me to sit for the examination.
5. With short adjectives		
до́лжен ра́д гото́в и т.д.	Я до́лжен занима́ться мно́го. Ja dólzhen zanimát'sja mnógo. या दोल्ज्झन ज़नीमात्स्या म्नोगा। I must study a lot.	Я до́лжен прийти́ к ва́м. Ja dólzhen prijtí k vám. या दोल्ज्झन प्रीइची क वाम। I must come to you.
	Я ра́д ви́деть ва́с здоро́вым. Ja rád vídet' vás zdoróvym. या राद विजेच वास ज्दारोविम। I am glad to see you healthy.	Я ра́д познако́миться с ва́ми. Ja rád poznakómit'sja s vámi. या राद पज़्नाकोमित्स्या स्वामी। I am glad to meet you.
	Я всегда́ гото́в помога́ть ва́м. Ja vsegdá gotóv pomogát' vám. या व्सिगदा गतोफ पमागाच वाम। I am always ready to help you.	Я гото́в помо́чь ва́м. Ja gotóv pomóch' vám. या गतोफ पमोछ वाम। I am ready to help you.

The Adjective

Adjectives indicate feature, property, quality, i.e. specify objects, persons. Adjectives possess full and short forms. For example:

Во́т како́й краси́вый сто́л!
Vót kakój krasívyj stól!
वोत काकोय क्रास्व्यिी स्तोल।
What a beautiful table!

Э́тот сто́л краси́в.
Jétot stól krasív.
एतत स्तोल क्रासिव।
This table is beautiful.

Full adjectives reply to questions:
како́й? kakój? *кака́я?* kakája? *како́е?* kakóe? *каки́е?* kakíe?
काकोय? ककाया? काकोये? काकीये?
(What kind of?/ Which type of?)

Short adjectives answer the questions:
како́в? kakóv? какова́? kaková?каково́? kakovó? каковы́? kakový?
काकोव? काकोवा? काकोवो? काकोवी?
Brevity or fullness of adjective is specified by the part which an adjective takes in the sentence.

(a) Full Adjectives

Full adjectives undergo changes depending on genders, numbers and cases but they do not have independent forms. Forms of gender, number and case depend on forms of nouns or pronouns. In the plural adjectives possess one single form for all genders. Function of full adjectives – definition (attribute) or predicate (component, composing, constituent part of nominal predicate).

Мы́ купи́ли интере́сные кни́ги.

Mý kupíli interésnye knígi.

We bought interesting books.

Э́ти кни́ги интере́сные.

Jéti knígi interésnye.

These books are interesting.

Gender and Number of Adjectives

Gender	Singular number како́й? кака́я? како́е?	Plural number какие?		
Masculine number	како́й вра́ч? но́вый како́й теа́тр? ру́сский	каки́е	вра́чи теа́тры кни́ги пе́сни зда́ния слова́	НО́ВЫЕ РУ́ССКИЕ
Feminine number	кака́я кни́га? но́вая кака́я пе́сня? ру́сская			
Neuter number	како́е зда́ние? но́вое како́е сло́во? ру́сское			

While changing in genders, numbers and cases adjectives may have variations in endings. Selection of one of the variations depends on the stem of an adjective. The following types of stems are distinguished: a) hard -terminating in hard consonant; b) soft - terminating in soft consonant; c) terminating in - г, к, х; d) terminating in - ж, ш, ч, щ.

Types of Full Adjective Stems

Gender	Hard stem	Soft stem	Stem ending in Щ,Ш, Ж, Ч	Stem ending in Г, К, Х	Endings
Masculine number	но́вый -new молодо́й – young	ле́тний - summer	хоро́ший -good большо́й - big	ру́сский -Russian доро́гой -expensive	ЫЙ. ИЙ, ОЙ,
Neuter number	но́вое молодо́е	Ле́тнее	хоро́шее большо́е	ру́сское дорого́е	ОЕ, ЕЕ
Feminine number	но́вая молода́я	Ле́тняя	хоро́шая больша́я	ру́сская дорога́я	АЯ, ЯЯ
Plural number	но́вые молоды́е	Ле́тние	хоро́шие больши́е	ру́сские дороги́е	ЫЕ, ИЕ

- Adjectives of Masculine gender have the ending ОЙ – which is accented большо́й, сухо́й, живо́й, дорого́й.
- Adjectives of the Neuter gender with stems terminating in Ж, Ч, Ш, Щ have endings ОЕ accented and ЕЕ - which is unaccented. большо́е, хоро́шее.
- In the plural adjectives possess one single form for all endings -ЫЕ, ИЕ.

Case system of full adjectives

Case	Question	Masculine and Neuter gender	Singular number	Ending
Nom.	како́й? како́е?	но́вый хоро́ший голубо́й большо́й но́вое хоро́шее голубо́е большо́е	ле́тний ру́сский ле́тнее ру́сское	ЫЙ, ИЙ,ОЙ ОЕ, ЕЕ
Gen.	како́го?	но́вого хоро́шего голубо́го большо́го	ле́тнего ру́сского	ОГО, ЕГО
Dat.	како́му?	но́вому хоро́шему голубо́му большо́му	ле́тнему ру́сскому	ОМУ, ЕМУ
Inst.	каки́м?	но́вым хоро́шим голубы́м больши́м	ле́тним ру́сским	ЫМ, ИМ
Prep.	о како́м?	но́вом хоро́шем голубо́м большо́м	ле́тнем ру́сском	ОМ, ЕМ

CHAPTER

4 Tells us About Your Family

1.	челове́к	Chelovék	छिलावेक	Human Being
2.	же́нщина	zhénshhina	ज्झेनशिना	woman
3.	мужчи́на	muzhchína	मूशिना	man
4.	молодо́й челове́к	molodój chelovék	मलादोई छिलावेक	young man
5.	де́вушка	dévushka	जेवूशका	girl (in her late teens)
6.	ма́льчик	mál'chik	मालछीक	boy
7.	де́вочка	dévochka	जेवचका	(small) girl
8.	Семья́	Sem'já	सिमया	Family
9.	жена	zhená	जिना	wife
10.	му́ж	múzh	मूज्झ	husband
11.	ма́ть	mát'	माच	mother
12.	оте́ц	otéts	अचेयत्स	father
13.	до́чь	dóch'	दोछ	daughter
14.	сы́н	sýn	सीन	son
15.	сестра́	sestra	सीस्त्रा	sister
16.	бра́т	brát	ब्रात	brother
17.	роди́тели (*pl*).	rodíteli	राजीचेली	parents
18.	де́душка	dédushka	जेदूशका	grandfather
19.	ба́бушка	bábushka	बावूशका	grandmother
20.	вну́к	vnúk	वनूक	grandson
21.	вну́чка	vnúchka	वनूचका	grandaughter

22.	дя́дя	djádja	जयाजया	uncle
23.	тётя	tjotja	चियोचया	aunt
24.	племя́нник	plemjánnik	प्लीमयानिक	nephew
25.	племя́нница	plemjánnitsa	प्लीमयानित्सा	niece

Parts of the Body

1.	голова́	golová	गलावा	Head
2.	шея́	shejá	शेया	Neck
3.	ло́б	lóp	लोप	Forehead
4.	лицо́	litsó	लित्सो	Face
5.	гла́з	gláz	ग्लास	Eye
6.	но́с	nós	नोस	Nose
7.	ро́т	rót	रोत	Mouth
8.	гу́бы	gúby	गुबि	*pl.* Lips
9.	зу́б	zúp	ज़ूप	Tooth
10.	у́хо	úkho	उखा	Ear
11.	го́рло	górlo	गोरला	Throat
12.	во́лосы	vólosy	वोलसी	pl. hair
13.	рука	ruká	रुका	arm, hand
14.	па́лец	pálets	पालेत्स	finger, toe
15.	нога́	nogá	नगा	foot, leg
16.	спина́	spiná	स्पिना	Back

DIALOGUE - 1

Э́то вся́ моя́ семья́. Э́то мо́й оте́ц.

Jéto vsjá mojá sem'já. Jéto mój otéts.

एता व्सया मया सीमिया। एता मोइ अचियतस।

This is my entire family. This is my father.

А э́то кто́? Твоя́ ма́ть?

A jéto któ? Tvojá mát'?

आ एता कतो? तवया माच?

And who is this? Your mother?

Не́т, э́то моя́ ба́бушка. Она́ была́ учи́тельницей. Спра́ва — оте́ц.

Nét ,jéto mojá bábushka. Oná býla uchítel'nitsej. Správa — otéts.

नीयत एता मया बाबूशका। अना बिला उछिचेलनित्सये। स्प्रावा अतछीयतस।

No, this is my grandmother. She was a school teacher. On the right is my father.

Э́то, наве́рное, тво́й бра́т и́ли племя́нник. О́н похо́ж на́ тебя́. Бе́рно?

Jéto, navérnoe, tvój brát íli plemjánnik. Ón pokhózh ná tebjá.Vérno?

एता नावेयरना तवोई ब्रात इली पलेमयानिक। ओन पोखोज न चिबया। वेयरना?

This is perhaps your brother or nephew. He resembles you. Am I right?

Пра́вильно. Мла́дший бра́т. О́н сейча́с конча́ет шко́лу.

Právil'no. Mládshij brát. Ón sejchás koncháet shkólu.

प्राविलना, मलादशी ब्रात। ओन सिछ्यास कनछायित शकोलू।

Right. He is my younger brother. He is presently completing his school.

А э́то твоя́ ма́ть?

A jéto tvojá mát'?

आ एता त्वया माच?

And this is your mother?

Не́т, тётя.

Nét, tjotja.

नियत चयोचया।

No, aunt.

О́чень краси́вая же́нщина.

Óchen' krasívaja zhénshhina.

ओछिन करासिवया जेनशिना।

She is a very pretty woman.

Она́ Вра́ч. Сейча́с у́же на́ пе́нсии.

Oná Vrách. Sejchás úzhe ná pénsii.

अना व्राच। शिचयास उजे ना पेनसी,।

She is a doctor. Now she is retired.

DIALOGUE - 2

Отве́тьте, пожа́луйста, на́ вопро́сы. Я запо́лню ва́шу анкету.

Otvét'te, pozhálujsta, ná voprósy. Ja zapólnju váshu ankétu.

अतवेचे पजालूसता न वापरोसी। या जापलनियू वाशू अंकेतू।

Please, answer the questions. I will fill up your application form.

Та́к, и́мя и фами́лию я у́же зна́ю. Когда́ и где́ вы́ родили́сь?

Ták, ímja i famíliju ja úzhe znáju. Kogdá i gdé vý rodilís'?

ताक ईमिया इ फामिलूयू य्रा उजे जनायूँ। कगदा वि रजीलीस?

So, I already know your name and surname. When and where were you born?

Я роди́лся (-а́сь) в 1975 году́, в го́роде Кли́вленде, шта́т Пенсильва́ния.

Ja rodílsja (-ás’) v 1975 godú, v górode Klívlende, shtát Pensil’vánija.

या रजीलीस्या (रजीलस) व 1975 गद् व गोरजय कलीवलनजेय, शतात पैनिसिलवानिया।

I was born in 1975, in Cleveland city in the state of Pennsylvania.

Ка́к зову́т ва́ших отца́ и ма́ть? Че́м они́ занима́ются?

Kák zovút váshikh otsaá i mát’? Chém oní zanimájutsja?

काक जावुत वाशिख अतसा इ माच? छेयम अनी जनीमायूत्स्या?

What is the name of your father and mother? What are their professions?

Моего́ отца́ зову́т Сти́в По́ртер, о́н коммерса́нт. Мою́ ма́ть зову́т Ма́рия. Она́ домохозя́йка.

Moegó otsaá zovút Stív Pórter, ón kommersánt. Mojú mát’ zovút Márija. Oná domokhozjájka.

मायेवो अतसा जावुत स्टीव पोरटर, ओन कमेरसात। मयू माच जावुत मारिया। अना दमा खजयायिका।

My father’s name is Steve Potter, he is a businessman. My mother’s name is Maria. She is a house wife.

Е́сть ли́ у ва́с бра́тья и сестры́?

Ést’ lí u vás brát’ja i sestrý?

यस्त ली उवास ब्रात्य इ सिस्त्री?

Do you have brothers and sisters?

У меня́ е́сть сестра́ и бра́т. Сестру́ зову́т Кэ́т, ей 9 ле́т, она́ ещё учи́тся в шко́ле. Бра́та зову́т Ро́берт, ему́ 22 го́да, о́н учи́тся в университе́те.

U menjá ést' sestrá i brát. Sestrú zovút Kjét, ej 9 lét, oná eshhjo uchítsja v shkóle. Bráta zovút Róbert, emú 22 góda, ón uchítsja v universitéte.

उ मिनया यस्त सिस्त्रा ई ब्रात। सिस्त्रू जावूत केत, यई 9 लियत, अना इशो उछीतस्या व शकोले, ब्राता जावुत रोबट, ईमू 22 गोदा ओन उछीतस्या व उनीवैरसिचयचे।

I have a sister and a brother. My sister's name is Kate, she is 9 years old, and she is a school girl. My brother's name is Robert, he is 22 years old. He studies in the university.

Вы́ жена́ты (за́мужем)?	Are you married?
Vý zhenáty (zámuzhem)?	वी जिनाती (जामुजिम)?
Не́т, я не́ жена́т (незаму́жнем).	No, I'm single.
Nét, ja né zhenát (nezamúzhnem).	नीयत या नीजिनात (नी जामुजेम)
Моя́ жена́ - учи́тельница.	My wife is a teacher.
Mojá zhená - uchítel'nitsa.	मया जिना उछीचलनितसा।
Она́ развела́сь со свои́м му́жем.	She divorced her husband.
Oná razvelás' so svoím múzhem.	अना रजविलास स स्वंइम मूजम।

О́БА ма́льчика, о́кна   О́БЕ де́вочки, кни́ги

О́БА means both. It changes with gender.

One may ask such questions concerning age:

Мне́	15 ... 20 ле́т
Ему́	
Ей	21, 31 ... го́д
Ско́лько	32, 43, 24 ... го́да

Отцу́ ле́т? НО́: (приме́рно, приблизи́тельно)
Ма́тери ле́т 15—16
го́да 32—33

В како́м го́ду вы родили́сь?

V kakóm gódu vý rodilís'?

व काकोम गदू वि रजीलीस?

When were you born?

Я роди́лся в 1975 (ты́сяча девятьсо́т се́мьдесят пя́том) году.

Ja rodílsja v 1975 (týsjacha devjat'sót sém'desjat pjátom) godú.

या रजीलीस्या व तीसेछा जेवितसोत सेमजेस्त पयातम गदू।

I was born in 1975.

Ва́ш го́д рожде́ния? Како́в ва́ш во́зраст?

Vásh gód rozhdénija? Kakóv vásh vózrast?

वाश गोद रजजेनिया? काकोव वाश वोज्रस्त।

Your year of birth? What is your age?

1975 (ты́сяча девятьсо́т се́мьдесят пя́тый) го́д.

týsjacha devjat'sót sém'desjat pjáty got.

तीसेछा जेवितसोत सेमजेस्त पयाती गोत।

1975.

Мне́ два́дцать три́ го́да.

I am twenty three years old.

मीनिये दावदसच त्री गोदा।

The Accusative case of Nouns

Gender	Nominative	Accusative sing.	Accusative pl.
		ви́жу, люблю́, Кого́? **Что́?**	
Masculine	оте́ц го́сть самова́р фи́льм	отца́ го́стя самова́р фи́льм	отцо́в гостье́й самова́ры фи́льмы
Feminine	сестра́ де́вушка дере́вня аудито́рия	сестру́ де́вушку дере́вню аудито́рию	сестёр де́вушек дере́вни аудито́рии
Neuter	окно́ по́ле зда́ние	окно́ по́ле зда́ние	о́кна поля́ зда́ния

The Dative case of Nouns

Gender	Nominative	Dative sing.	Dative pl.
		Кому́? Чему́?	
Masculine	оте́ц го́сть самова́р фи́льм	отцу́ го́стю самова́ру фи́льму	отца́м гостя́м самова́рам фи́льмам
Feminine	сестра́ де́вушка дере́вня аудито́рия	сестре́ де́вушке дере́вне аудито́рии	сестра́м де́вушкам дере́вням аудито́риям
Neuter	окно́ по́ле зда́ние	окну́ по́лю зда́нию	о́кнам поля́м зда́ниям

CHAPTER

5 Number, Dates and Time

Numerals

	Cardinals		Ordinals	
1.	оди́н	one	пе́рвый	first
	odín	अजीन	pérvyj	पेरवी
2.	два́	two	второ́й	second
	dvá	दवा	vtorój	व्तारोई
3.	три́	three	тре́тий	third
	trí	त्री	trétij	त्रेची
4.	четы́ре	four	четвёртый	fourth
	chetýre	छतीरेय	chetvjortyj	छितवियोरती
5.	пя́ть	five	пя́тый	fifth
	pját'	पयाज्च	pjátyj	पयाती
6.	ше́сть	six	шесто́й	sixth
	shést'	शेसत	shestój	शिसतोई
7.	се́мь	seven	седьмо́й	seventh
	sém'	सेम	sed'mój	सिदमोई
8.	во́семь	eight	восьмо́й	eighth
	vósem'	वोसिम	vos'mój	वसमोई
9.	де́вять	nine	девя́тый	ninth
	dévjat'	जेविच	devjátyj	जिवयाती
10.	де́сять	ten	деся́тый	tenth
	désjat'	देसेच	desjátyj	दिसयाती
11.	оди́ннадцать	eleven	оди́ннадцатый	eleventh
	odínnadtsat'	अजीनातज	odínnadtsatyj	अजीनातसती

12.	две́надцать	twelve	две́надцатый	twelfth
	dvénadtsat’	द्विनातसच	dvénadtsatyj	द्विनातसती
13.	три́надцать	thirteen	три́надцатый	thirteenth
	trínadtsat’	त्रीनादसच	trínadtsatyj	त्रीनोदसती
14.	четы́рнадцать	fourteen	четы́рнадцатый	fourteenth
	chetýrnadtsat’	छितीरचनादसच	chetýrnadtsatyj	छितीरनादसती
15.	пятна́дцать	fifteen	пятна́дцатый	fifteenth
	pjatnádtsat’	पितनातसज	pjatnádtsatyj	पितनादसती
16.	шестна́дцать	sixteen	шестна́дцатый	sixteenth
	shestnádtsat’	शिसनातसज	shestnádtsatyj	शिसनादसती
17.	семна́дцать	seventeen	семна́дцатый	seventeenth
	semnádtsat’	सिमनादसच	semnádtsatyj	सिमनादसती
18.	восемна́дцать	eighteen	восемна́дцатый	eighteenth
	vosemnádtsat’	वसीमनादसच	vosemnádtsatyj	वसीमनादसती
19.	девятна́дцать	nineteen	девятна́дцатый	nineteenth
	devjatnádtsat’	जीवितनादसच	devjatnádtsatyj	जीवितनादसती
20.	два́дцать	twenty	двадца́тый	twentieth
	dvádtsat’	दावदसच	dvadtsátyj	दवादसाती
30.	три́дцать	thirty	тридца́тый	thirtieth
	trídtsat’	त्रीदतसच	tridtsátyj	त्रीदतसाती
40.	со́рок	forty	сороково́й	fortieth
	sórok	सोरक	sorokovój	सरकावोई
50.	пятьдеся́т	fifty	пятидеся́тый	fiftieth
	pjat’desját	पिजिस्यितत	pjatidesjátyj	पिजिजिस्याती
60.	шестьдеся́т	sixty	шестидеся́тый	sixtieth
	shest’desját	शेचिस्यात	shestidesjátyj	शिसतिजिस्याती
70.	семьдеся́т	seventy	семидеся́тый	seventieth
	sem’desját	सेमजिस्यत	semidesjátyj	सेमीजिस्याती
80.	во́семьдесят	eighty	восьмидеся́тый	eightieth
	vósem’desjat	वोसिमजिस्यत	vos’midesjátyj	वस्मीजस्याती

90.	девяно́сто	ninety	девяно́стый	ninetieth
	devjanósto	जिवेनोस्ता	devjanóstyj	जिवेनोस्तनी
100.	сто́	hundred	со́тый	hundredth
	stó	सतो	sótyj	सोती
	Zero is но́ль. nól’. नोल			

Russian words for Date and Time

Days of the week			
понеде́льник	ponedél’nik	पनीजेलनिक	Monday
вто́рник	vtórnik	फतोरिनिक	Tuesday
среда́	sredá	स्रीदा	Wednesday
четве́рг	chetvérg	छितव्रेक	Thursday
пя́тница	pjátnitsa	पयातनितसा	Friday
суббо́та	subbóta	सुबोता	Saturday
воскресе́нье	voskreseìn’e	वसेक्रसेनिय	Sunday

Months			
янва́рь	janvár’	यनवार	January
февра́ль	fevrál’	फेवराल	February
ма́рт	márt	र्मात	March
апре́ль	aprél’	अपरैल	April
ма́й	máj	माई	May
ию́нь	ijún’	ईयूण	June
ию́ль	ijúl’	ईयूल	July
а́вгуст	ávgust	आवगुस्त	August
сентя́брь	sentjábr’	सिंत्यबर	September
октя́брь	oktjábr’	अकत्याबर	October
ноя́брь	nojábr’	नयाबर	November
дека́брь	dekábr’	जैकाबर	December

Common words			
сего́дня	segódnja	सीवोदनिया	today
за́втра	závtra	जाफतरा	tomorrow
по́слезавтра	póslezavtra	पोसले जाफतरा	day after tomorrow
вчера́	vcherá	व्फछेरा	yesterday
позавчера́	pozavchera	पजवछीरा	day before yesterday
у́тро	útro	ऊतरा	morning
де́нь	dén’	जेन	day
но́чь	nóch’	नोछ	night
у́тром	útrom	उतरम	in the morning
днём	dnjom	दन्योम	in the afternoon
ве́чером	vécherom	वेछेरम	in the evening
но́чью	nóch’ju	नोछ्यू	at night
секу́нда	sekúnda	सिकूंदा	second
мину́та	minúta	मिनूता	minute
ча́с	chás	छास	hour
неде́ля	nedélja	निजेल	week
ме́сяц	mésjats	मेस्तिस	month
го́д	gód	गोत	year

Скажи́те, пожа́луйста, кото́рый ча́с?
Skazhíte, pozhálujsta, kotóryj chás?
साकाजिचे पजालूसता कातोरी छास?
What’s the time, please?

Пя́ть часо́в.
Pját’ chasóv.
पयाच छिसोव।
It’s five o’clock.

Ро́вно ше́сть часо́в.
Róvno shést’ chasóv.
रोवना शेसत छिसोव।
It’s exactly six.

Полови́на четвёртого.
Polovína chetvjortogo.
पलाविना छितवयोरतवा।
It’s half past three.

Пятна́дцать мину́т тре́тьего.
Pjatnádtsat’ minút trét’ego.
पितनादसच मिनूत त्रेचेवा।
It’s a quarter past two.

Бе́з пяти́ се́мь.
Béz pjatí sém’.
बिज पिची सेम।
It’s five to seven.

Пя́ть мину́т восьмо́го.
Pját’ minút vos’mógo.
पयाच मिनूत वसमोवा।
It’s five past seven.

Не́ скаже́те мне́ то́чное вре́мя?
Né skazhéte mné tóchnoe vrémja?
नि स्काजिचे मिनिये तोचछनेय व्रेमिया?
Could you tell me the right time, please?

Ско́лько вре́мени?
Skól’ko vrémeni?
स्कोलका व्रेमिनी?
What time is it?

Двена́дцать часо́в дня́ (но́чи).
Dvenádtsat' chasóv dnjá (nóchi).
दवेनातसच छिसोव दनया (नोछी)।
It's twelve noon (midnight).

У́же де́вять часо́в?
Úzhe dévjat' chasóv?
उजे जेविच छिसोव?
Is it nine already?

Мои́ часы́ отста́ют (спеша́т) на де́сять мину́т.
Moí chasý otstájut (speshát) na désjat' minút.
मई छिसी अतस्तायूत (सपेशात)।
My watch is ten minutes slow (fast).

Мои́ часы́ останови́лись.
Moí chasý ostanovílis'.
मई छिसी अस्तानाविलिस।
My watch has stopped.

У на́с мно́го вре́мени.
U nás mnógo vrémeni.
उनास/मनोगा व्रेमिनीं।
We have plenty of time.

Сего́дня о́н опаздыва́ет.
Segódnja ón opazdyváet.
सिवोद्यनिया ओन अपाजदीवयत।
He's late today.

Я не́ сли́шком ра́но?
Ja né slíshkom ráno?
या नि स्लीषकम राणा?
Am I too early?

Вы́ опозда́ли.
Vý opozdáli.
वी अपजदाली।
You're late.

Потороопите́сь!
Potoropités'!
पतरापिचेस!
Hurry up!

Бы́стрее!
Býstree!
बिस्त्रेई!
Be quick!

Како́е сего́дня число́?
Kakóe segódnja chisló?
काकोए सिवोदनिया छिसलो?
What's the date today?

Како́е вчера́ бы́ло число́?
Kakóe vcherá býlo chisló?
काकोए व्छिरा बिला छिसलो?
What was the date yesterday?

Сего́дня - тре́тье ма́я.
Segódnja - trét'e mája.
सिवोदानिया त्रेचेई माया
Today is the third of May.

Како́й сего́дня де́нь неде́ли?
Kakój segódnja dén' nedéli?
काकोई सिवोदानिया जेन निजेली?
What's today?

Сего́дня понеде́льник.
Segódnja ponedél'nik.
सिवोदानिया पनेजेलनिक।
Today is Monday.

This is how the Russians usually tell the Time

15.05 пя́ть мину́т четвёртого
pját' minút chetvjortogo
पयाच मिनूत छितव्योरतवा

3.10 де́сять мину́т четвёртого
désjat' minút chetvjortogo
जेसेच मिनूत छितवयोरतवा

3.15 пятна́дцать мину́т четвёртого
pjatnádtsat' minút chetvjortogo
पितनादसच मिनूत छितवयोरतवा

3.20 два́дцать мину́т четвёртого
dvádtsat' minút chetvjortogo
दवादस्च मिनूत छितवयोरतवा

15.25 два́дцать пя́ть четвёртого
dvádtsat' pját' chetvjortogo
दवादस्च पयाच मिनूत छितवयोरतवा

3.30 полови́на четвёртого
polovína chetvjortogo
पलावीना छितवयोरतवा

3.35 без двадцати пяти́ четыре
béz dvádtsati pjatí chetýre
बिज दवादसची पिची छतीरीय

15.40 бéз двáдцати четы́ре
béz dvádtsati chetýre
बिज दवादसची पिची छतीरीय

3.45 бéз пятнáдцати (бéз чéтверти) четы́ре
béz pjatnádtsati (béz chétverti) chetýre
बिज पितनादसची (बिज छेतवेयरती) छतीरीय

3.50 бéз дéсяти четы́ре
béz désjati chetýre
विज जिसेची छतीरीय

3.55 бéз пяти́ четы́ре
béz pjatí chetýre
विज पिची छतीरीय

This is how they speak on the Radio

7.10 сéмь часóв дéсять мину́т
sém' chasóv désjat' minút
सेम छिसोव जेसित मिनूत

7.30 сéмь часóв три́дцать мину́т
sém' chasóv trídcat' minút
सेम छिसोव त्रीदसच मिनूत

7.45 сéмь часóв сóрок пять мину́т
sém' chasóv sórok pját' minút
सेम छिसोव सोरक पयाच मिनूत

13.15 тринáдцать часóв пятнáдцать мину́т
trinádtsat' chasóv pjatnádcat' minút
त्रीनादसच छिसोव पिजिस्यात मिनूत

13.55 трина́дцать часо́в пятьдеся́т пя́ть мину́т
trinádtsat' chasóv pjat'desját pját' minút
त्रीनादसच छिसोव पिजिस्यात पयाच मिनूत

Сейча́с ро́вно ча́с	Sejchás róvno chás
Right now it is exactly one o'clock	सिछयास रोवना छास
два́ часа́	dvá chasá
two o'clock	दवा छिसा
три́ часа́	trí chasá
three o'clock	त्री छिसा
четы́ре часа́	chetýre chasá
four o'clock	छतीरिय छिसा
пя́ть часо́в	pját' chasóv
five o'clock	पयाच छिसोव
ше́сть часо́в	shést' chasóv
six o'clock	शेसत छिसोव
се́мь часо́в	sém' chasóv
seven o'clock	सेम छिसोव
во́семь часо́в	vósem' chasóv
eight o'clock	वोसीम छिसोव
де́вять часо́в	dévjat' chasóv
nine o'clock	जेविच छिसोव
де́сять часо́в	désjat' chasóv
ten o'clock	जेसिच छिसोव

одиннадцать часов odínnadtsat' chasóv
eleven o'clock अजीनातसच छिसोव

двенадцать часов dvenádtsat' chasov
twelve o'clock (mid day or midnight) दवेनातसच छिसोव

Который час? Сколько (сейчас) времени? Kotóriy chás? Skól'ko (syeychás) vryémyeni?/What time is it?

Сейчас час; два, ... часа; пять, ... часов.

(Till 30 minutes past the hour):

Сейчас десять минут первого; четверть (пятнадцать минут) четвёртого; половина восьмого.

(After 30 minutes to the next hour):

Сейчас без пяти (минут) четыре; без четверти (без пятнадцати минут) четыре; без двадцати пяти (минут) восемь.

Note:

In some cases, *e.g.*, on the radio, on trains, etc., the time is given in an official, non-conversational way, using the 24-hour clock:

13.05 тринадцать часов пять минут;
trínadtsat' chasóv pját' minút
त्रिनादसच छिसोव पयाच मिनूत

7.35 семь часов тридцать пять минут.
sém' chasóv trídtsat' pját' minút..
सेम छिसोव त्रिदसच पयाच मिनूत

2. Когда́? В кото́ром часу́? Kogdá? V kotórom chasoó?

कगदा? व कतोरम छिसू

At what time?

1. Па́вел обеда́ет в ча́с.
Pável obedáet v chás.
पाविल अबेदयत व छास
Pavel has dinner at one.

О́н прихо́дит домо́й в четы́ре часа́.
Ón prikhódit domój v chetýre chasá.
ओन प्रिखोजित दामोई व छतीरीय छिसा
He comes home at four.

Мы́ ужина́ем в се́мь часо́в.
Mý uzhináem v sém' chasóv.
मी उजीनयम व सेम छीसोव
We have supper at seven.

2. Сего́дня о́н пришёл домо́й че́тверть пя́того.
Segódnja ón prishjol domój chétvert' pjátogo.
सीवोदनिया ओन प्रिशयोल दामोई छेतवेरच पयातवा
Today he came home at a quarter past four.

Они́ ужина́ют в полови́не восьмо́го.
Oní uzhinájut v polovíne vos'mógo.
अनी उजीनयूत व पलावीने वसमोवा।
They have supper at half past seven.

3. Па́вел пошёл обеда́ть бе́з пяти́ ча́с.
Pável poshjol obedát' béz pjatí chás.
पाविल पाशयोल अबैयदच बिज पिची छास।
Pavel went to dinner at five to one.

О́н пришёл домо́й бе́з че́тверти четы́ре.
Ón prishjol domój béz chétverti chetýre.
ओन प्रिशोयल दामोई बिज छेतवेयरची छतीरीय।
He came home at a quarter to four.

Сего́дня мы́ се́ли ужина́ть бе́з два́дцати пяти́ во́семь.
Segódnja mý séli uzhinát' béz dvádtsati pjatí vósem'.
सिवोदनिया मी सिएेली उजीनछ बिज दावदसदची पिची वोसीम।
We sat down to supper at twenty-five to eight.

B. Sometimes the time of the day is added:
Э́то бы́ло в три́ часа́ но́чи.
Jéto býlo v trí chasá nóchi.
एता बिला व त्री छिसा नोछी।
This happened at three in the morning.

О́н прие́хал в ше́сть часо́в ве́чера.
Ón priékhal v shést' chasóv véchera.
ओ प्रियेखल व शेषत् छिसोव वेछेरा।
He came at six in the evening.

The period from 5 to 11 is considered as morning
(с 5 пять часо́в у́тра до 11 одиннадцать часо́в у́тра),
12—16 — afternoon (с 12 двенадцать часо́в дня до 4 четыре часо́в дня́),

17—23 — evening

(с 5 пять часо́в ве́чера до 11 одиннадцать часо́в ве́чера),

24—4 — night

(с 12 двенадцать часо́в но́чи до 4 четыре часо́в но́чи).

B. 1. О́коло дву́х часо́в(gen.)

Ókolo dvúkh chasóv.

ओकला दूव्ख छिसोव।

At about two o'clock.

2. По́сле дву́х часо́в(gen.)

Pósle dvúkh chasóv.

पोसले दूव्ख छिसोव।

After two o'clock.

3. Чере́з два́ часа́ (acc.)

Cheréz dvá chasá.

छिरीज दवा छिसा।

In two hours (time).

4. К дву́м часа́м (dat.)

K dvúm chasám.

क दूम छिसाम।

By two o'clock.

5. За два часа́ (acc.)

до (+ gen.) Za dva chasá.

जा दवा छिसा।

Two hours before.

3. Ка́к до́лго? Ско́лько вре́мени?
Kák dólgo? Skól'ko vryémyeni?

काक दोलगा ? सकोलका व्रेमिनी ?

How long?

1 Два́ часа́ (For) two hours

(По́сле заня́тий о́н отды́хал два́ часа́).

Pósle zanjátij ón otdýkhal dvá chasá.

पोसले जनयाची ओन अदिखाल दवाछिसा।

After the classes he rested for two hours.

2 С дву́х до трёх From two to three (o'clock)

स दूव्ख द त्रियोख

(По́сле заня́тий о́н отды́хал с дву́х до трёх часо́в).

Pósle zanjátij ón otdýkhal s dvúkh do trjokh chasóv.

पोसले जनयाची ओन आदिखाल स दूव्ख द त्रियोख छिसोव।

After the classes he rested from two to three o'clock.

Часы́ идут то́чно

Chasý idut tóchno

छिसी ईदूत तोछना

My watch is right.

Часы́ спеша́т, отста́ют

Chasý speshát, otstájut

छिसी स्पेशात, अतस्तायूत

My watch is fast, slow.

На́ мои́х (часа́х) три́

Ná moíkh (chasákh) trí

ना मईख (छिसाक) त्री

It's three by my watch.

Проверя́ть, провери́ть часы́
Proverját', proverít' chasý
प्रावेरयाच, प्रावेरीच छिसी
to check a watch.

Ста́вить, поста́вить часы́
Stavit', postavit' chasý
सताविच, पसताविच छिसी
to set a watch, a clock.

CHAPTER

6 Shop

Where things can be bought?

1.	Продово́льственный Мага́зин	Grocery Store
	Prodovól'stvennyj Magázin	प्रदावोलसतविनी मगाजिन
2.	Универса́льный Мага́зин (Универса́м)	Supermarket
	Universál'nyj Magázin (Universám)	उनीवरेसालनी (उनीविरसाम) मगाजिन
3.	Универма́г	Departmental store
	Univermág	उनीवेरमाग
4.	Покупа́тель (-и)	Buyer(S)
	Pokupátel'	पकूपाचेल
5.	Продаве́ц (-цы)	Seller(S)
	Prodavets	प्रदाव्यत्स
6.	Продава́ть/Прода́ть	To Sell
	Prodavat'/Prodat'	प्रदावाच/प्रदाच
7.	Покупа́ть/Купи́ть	To Buy
	Pokupat'/Kupit'	पकूपाच/कूपिच
8.	Плати́ть/Заплати́ть	To Pay
	Platit'/Zaplatit'	पलाचीच/जापलाचीच

9.	Ры́нок	Market
	Rynok	रीनक
10.	Ка́сса, Касси́р	Cash Counter; Cashier
	Kassa, Kassir	कासा, कासीर
11.	Сто́ить, Сто́имость	To Cost; Cost
	Stoit', Stoimost'	स्तोईच, स्तोईमस्त
12.	О́чередь	Queue/ Line
	Ochered'	ओछेरेज
13.	Ста́ть в о́чередь	To Get into A Line
	Stat' v ochered'	स्ताच' व ओछेरेज

Килогра́мм (апельси́нов, помидо́ров, колба́сы, соси́сок...)

Kilogramm (apel'sinov, pomidorov, kolbasy, sosisok….)

किलाग्राम (अपलसीनव, पमीदोरव, कलबासी, ससीस्क)

A kilo(gram) of (oranges, tomatoes, salami, sausages…)

По́лкилограмма (по́лкило) сы́ра, масла́, сахара́,...

Polkilogramma (polkilo) syra, masla, sakhara

पोलकिलाग्रामा (पोलकिलो) सीरा, मासला, सारा

Half a kilo of (cheese, butter, sugar,…)

Ба́нка консе́рвов, майоне́за, ко́фе, варе́ния, компо́та, помидо́ров, огурцо́в.

Banka konservov, majoneza kofe, varenija, kompota, pomidorov, ogurtsov.

ब्रांका कनसेरेवव, मेयोनिजा, कोफे, वारेनिया, कमपोता, पमीदोरव, अगूरत्सोव

A can of mayonnaise, coffee, jam, compote tomatoes, cucumbers.

Буты́лка молока́, минера́льной воды́, со́ка, вина́, подсо́лнечного масла́.

Butylka moloka, mineral'noj vody, soka, vina, podsolnechnogo masla.

बूतिलिका मलाका, मीनरालनेय वदी, सोका, वीना, पदसोलनिचनवा मासला।

A bottle of milk, mineral water, juice, wine, oil.

Коро́бка конфе́т, спи́чек, сигаре́т, со́ка.

Korobka konfet, spichek, sigaret, soka.

कारोबका कनफेत, स्पीछेक, सिगारेयत, सोका।

A box of chocolates, matches; a pack of cigarettes; a carton of juice.

Па́чка сахара́, со́ли, ко́фе, чая, пече́ния, сли́вочного масла́, сигаре́т.

Pachka sakhara, soli, kofe chaja, pechenija, slivochnogo masla, sigaret.

पाछका साखरा, सोली, कोफे, छाया, पिछेनिया, सीलवछनवा मासला, सीगारयत।

A packet of sugar, salt, coffee, tea, cookies, butter, cigarettes.

Пли́тка шокола́да.

Plitka shokolada.

पलीतका शकालादा।

A bar of chocolate.

Све́жий — несве́жий,

Svezhij — Nesvezhij

सवेजी, निसवेजी।

Fresh, Not Fresh,

Вчера́шний, Че́рствый (хлеб, бато́н,...).
vcherashnij, cherstvyj (khleb, baton,…).
छेराशनी, छेरस्तवी (खलेब, बातोन)
Yesterday-Made, Stale (bread).

Бе́лый, пшени́чный хлеб — чёрный, ржано́й хлеб.
Belyj, pshenichnyj khleb — chyornyj, rzhanoj khleb.
बेली, पिशेनिचनी खलेब – छियोरनी, रजानोई खलेब।
White bread, wheat bread — brown, rye bread.

Ве́щи.	Things/Goods.
veshhi	वेशी
Оде́жда.	Clothing.
Odezhda.	आजेशदा
О́бувь.	Footwear.
Obuv'.	ओबूफ

Разме́р пиджа́ка, ку́ртки, ту́фель...
Razmer pidzhaka, kurtki, tufel'…
रजमेयर पिदजाका, कूर्तकी, तूफेल
Size of a suit, jacket, shoes…

DIALOGUE - 1

А -Скажи́те, пожа́луйста, где здесь "Универма́г"?
Skazhite, pozhalujsta, gde zdes' "Univermag"?
शकाजीचे, पजालूसता गिजिय इजजियेस उनीवेरमाग?
Please tell me where is the departmental store?

Б - Иди́те пря́мо.

Idite prjamo.

इजीचे प्रयामा।

Go straight.

А -Э́то далеко́?

Jeto daleko?

ऐता दलेको?

Is it far?

Б - Да нет

Da net

दा नियत

No

А -Спаси́бо

Spasibo

स्पासिबा

Thank you

DIALOGUE - 2

А -Да́йте мне, пожа́луйста, оди́н бато́н.

Dajte mne, pozhalujsta, odin baton.

दायिचे मिनिये पजालूसता अजीन बातोन।

Please give me a loaf of bread.

Ско́лько сто́ит э́то коро́бка конфе́т?

Skol'ko stoit jeto korobka konfet? सकोलका स्तोईत एता कारोबका कनफेत?

How much does this box of sweets cost?

Б -Восемна́дцать рубле́й.

Vosemnadtsat' rublej.

वसीमनादसज रूबलिएई।

Eighteen rubles.

А - Да́йте мне коро́бку конфе́ты. Ещё ба́нку ко́фе и то́рт.

Dajte mne korobku konfety. Eshhjo banku kofe i tort.

दाईचे मिनिय कारोबकू कनफेती, इशो बांन्कु कोफे इ तोर्त।

lease give me a box of Sweets and a jar of coffee and cake.

Ско́лько всё э́то сто́ит?

Skol'ko vsjo jeto stoit?

सकोलका व्सयो एता सोईत?

How much does all this cost?

Б -Пятьдеся́т рубле́й.

Pjat'desjat rublej.

पिजिसियात रूबलेई।

Fifty rubles.

А -Вот сто рубле́й.

Vot sto rublej.

वोत छिर्तीनातसच रूबलेई।

Here are hundred rubles.

Б -Возьми́те сда́чу (change).

Voz'mite sdachu.

वजमिचेस्ज स्दाछू।

Please take the change.

А -Спаси́бо.

Spasibo.

स्पसीबा।

Thank you.

DIALOGUE - 3

А - Скажи́те, пожа́луйста, бу́лочки све́жие?

Skazhite, pozhalujsta, bulochki svezhie?

स्काजिचे पजालूसता बूलछकी स्वेजिये?

Please tell me, are these buns fresh?

Б - Вчера́шние.

Vcherashnie.

व्छेराशनिये।

They are yesterdays.

А - А бато́ны?

A batony?

आ! बातोनी?

And bread?

Б – Све́жие.

Svezhie.

शवेजिये।

It's fresh.

А - Да́йте мне, пожа́луйста, оди́н бато́н и ещё полови́нку чёрного хлеба.

Dajte mne, pozhalujsta, odin baton i eshhjo polovinku chyornogo khleba.

दाईचे मिनिये पज्झालूस्ता अजीन बातोन ई इशो पलाविनकू छोरनवा खेल्बा।

Please give me a loaf of white bread and half a loaf of rye bread.

1 (оди́н) рубль rubl’ (रूबल)

2 (два)
3 три,
4 четы́ре рубля rublja (रूबल्या)

5- 20 рубле́й, rublej (रूबल्ये)

But

21 рубль

32 рубля

58 рубле́й

100 рубле́й,

1000 рубле́й.....

The Genitive case of Nouns

Gender	Nominative	Genitive sing.	Accusative pl.
		Нет кого? Чего?	
Masculine	оте́ц	отц**а́**	отц**о́в**
	го́сть	го́ст**я**	гост**е́й**
	самова́р	самова́р**а**	самова́р**ов**
	фильм	фи́льм**а**	фи́льм**ов**
Feminine	сестра́	сестр**ы́**	Сестёр
	до́чь	до́чери	дочер**е́й**
	де́вушка	де́вушк**и**	де́вушек
	дере́вня	дере́вн**и**	дере́вн**и**
	аудито́рия	аудито́р**ии**	аудито́р**ии**
Neuter	окно́ по́ле	окна́ пол**я́**	окн**а́** пол**я́**
	зда́ние	зда́ни**я**	зда́ни**я**

The Instrumental case of Nouns

Gender	Nominative	Instrumental Sing.	Instrumental Pl.
		Быть кем? Чем?	
Masculine	оте́ц	отц**о́м**	отц**ами**
	го́сть	го́ст**ем**	гост**я́ми**
	самова́р	самова́р**ом**	самова́р**ами**
	фильм	фи́льм**ом**	фи́льм**ами**
Feminine	сестра́	сестр**о́й**	сёстр**ами**
	до́чь		
	де́вушка	де́вушк**ой**	де́вушк**ами**
	дере́вня	дере́вн**ей**	деревн**я́ми**
	аудито́рия	аудито́ри**ей**	аудито́ри**ями**
Neuter	окно́	окн**о́м**	о́кн**ами**
	по́ле	по́л**ем**	пол**я́ми**
	зда́ние	зда́ни**ем**	зда́ни**ями**

CHAPTER

7 Meals

1.	За́втрак – На за́втрак	Zavtrak – Na zavtrak
	Breakfast- For breakfast.	जाफत्रक — नाजाफत्रक
2.	За́втракать.	Zavtrakat’
	To have breakfast.	जाफतरकच
3.	Обе́д - На обе́д	Obed - Na obed
	Lunch — For lunch	अबेयद — ना अबेयद
4.	Обе́дать.	Obedat’
	To have lunch.	अबेयदच
5.	У́жин - На у́жин	Uzhin - Na uzhin
	Dinner — For dinner	उजीन — न उजीन
6.	У́жинать.	Uzhinat’
	To have dinner.	उजीनच
7.	Заку́ска(-и) – На заку́ску	Zakuska(-i) – Na zakusku
	Snack(s)	जाकूसका (ई) — ना जाकूसक
8.	Пе́рвое(-ые), Второ́е(-ые), Тре́тье(-ьи), блю́до(-а)-	Pervoe(-ye), Vtoroe(-ye), Tret’e(-’i), bljudo(-a)
	The first (second, third) course.	त्रेचे (ई), बलूद (आ)
9.	На пе́рвое, на второ́е, на тре́тье.	Na pervoe, na vtoroe, na tret’e
	For the 1st, 2nd, 3rd course.	ना पेरवए, ना फतारोऐ, ना त्रेचे
10.	На десе́рт	na desert
	For dessert	ना देर्सेत

11.	Еда́	Eda
	Meal, food	यदा
12.	Есть/Пое́сть	Est'/poest'
	To eat	येसत – पयेसत
13.	Ку́шать/Поку́шать	Kushat'/pokushat'
	To eat	कूशच – पकूशच
14.	Гото́вить/Пригото́вить	Gotovit'/prigotovit'
	To prepare, to cook, to make.	गातोविच – प्रिगातोविच
15.	Меню́	Menju
	Menu	मेनयु
16.	Официа́нт (-ы)	Ofitsiant (-y)
	Waiter	अफीतसान्त (ई)
17.	Счёт	Schyot
	Bill	शियोत

FOOD

со́ль	sol'	सोल	salt
мя́со	mjaso	मयासा	meat
ма́сло	maslo	मासला	butter
кефи́р	kefir	केफिर	kefir
молоко́	molokó	मलाको	milk
со́к	sók	सोक	juice
колбаса́	kolbasa	कलबासा	sausage
сы́р	sýr	सीर	cheese
яйцо́	jajtsó	यतसो	egg
ры́ба	ryba	रीबा	fish
карто́фель (*m*) (*coll.* карто́шка)	kartófel' kartóshka	करतोफिल (करतोशका)	potatoes
лу́к	lúk	लूक	onions
огурцы́	ogurtsy	अगुरत्सी	cucumbers

морко́вь (*f.*)	morkóv’	मरकोव	carrots
свёкла	svjokla	स्वयोकला	beet, beetroot
помидо́р	pomidór	पमीदोर	tomato
капу́ста	kapusta	कापूसता	cabbage
апельси́н	apel’sin	अपिलसीन	orange
я́блоко	jábloko	यबल्का	apple
виногра́д	vinograd	वीनाग्राद	grapes
конфе́ты	konfety	कनफेयती	sweets, candy
пиро́жные	pirózhnye	पिरोज्झनिये	pastries
то́рт	tórt	तोंत	cake

DIALOGUE - 1

В Ресторане
V Restorane
व स्तारानिये
In the Restaurant

Где здесь мо́жно пообе́дать?
Gde zdes’ mózhno poobedat’?
गिजिये जेस मोजना पअबेदच?
Where can we have lunch?

Недалеко́ отсю́да есть хоро́ший рестора́н.
Nedaleko otsjuda est’ khoroshij restoran.
निदलेको अतसूदा यस्त खारोशी रेस्तारान।
There is a good restaurant nearby.

До́брый ве́чер. Где мо́жно сесть?
Dóbryj vecher. Gde mózhno sest’?
दोबरी वेछर। गिजिये मोजना स्येस्त?
Good evening. Where can we sit?

Ва́с тро́е?

Vás tróe?

वास त्रोये?

There are three of you?

Да!

Da!

दा!

Yes!

Во́т меню. Что́ вы́ будете зака́зывать?

Vót menju. Chtó vý budete zakazyvat'?

वोत मेनयू। श्तो वी बूजीचे जकाजीवच?

Here is the menu. What would you like to order?

А что́ у ва́с е́сть и́з заку́сок?

A chtó u vás ést' íz zakúsok?

आ श्तो उवास येस्त इज जाकूसक?

What do you have for starters?

Сала́т мясно́й, сала́т и́з (кра́бов, помидо́ров, огурцо́в), (столи́чный, венегре́т) сала́т....

Salát mjasnój, salát íz (krábov, pomidórov, ogurtsóv), (stolíchnyj, venegrét) salát....

सलात मिस्नोई, सलात इज (क्राबफ्र, पमीदोरफ, अगूरत्सोफ) (स्तालीछनी, वेनेग्रेत) सलात.........

Meat salad, (crab, tomato, cucumber) salad, (stolychni, Russian) salad....

На пе́рвое:

Na pervoe:

ना पेरवयः

For the first course:

Щи́, бо́рщ, (овощно́й, ри́совый, фрукто́вый) су́п, уха́.

shhí,bórsh, (ovoshnój, risovyj, fruktóvyj) súp, ukha

शी, बोंश (अवशनोये, रीसावी, फ्रूकतोवी) सूप, उखा।

Schi, borsch, (vegetable, rice, fruit) soup, fish soup.

На второе: коле́ты по-ки́евски, ры́ба, жа́реная ку́рица.

Na vtoroe: kolety po-kievski, ryba, zharenaja kuritsa.

नाफतारोए – कतलियेती पकीवसकी, रीबा, जारेननाया-कूरीत्सा।

For the second course: Kievian cutlets, fish, and fried chicken.

И так, я бу́ду есть бо́рщ и сала́т "Столи́чный". А вы?

I tak, ja budu est' borshh i salat "Stolichnyj". A vy?

इ ताक या बुदू यस्त बोंश ई सलात स्तालिछनी। आ-वी?

So, I shall have Borsch and: stolichny" salad. How about you?

А я бу́ду щи и хлеб, пожа́луйста.

A ja budu shhi i khleb, pozhalujsta.

आ या वुदू शी ई खलेब पजालूसता।

And I will have schi and bread, please.

Я о́чень хочу́ пить.

Ja ochen' khochu pit'.

या ओछीन खाछू पीच।

I am very thirsty.

Предлага́ю вам компо́т.

Predlagaju vam kompót.

प्रीदलागायू वाम कमपोत।

I would recommend compote.

Спаси́бо.
Spasibo.
स्पसिबा।
Thank you.

Десе́рты: моро́женое, фру́кты, то́рт, пиро́жное.
Deserty: morózhenoe, frukty, tórt, pirózhnoe.
दिसयरती – मारोजनेय, फ्रूकती, तोरत, पिरोजनेय।
Desserts: ice- cream, fruits, cake, pastry.

Напи́тки : вода́, ча́й, ко́фе, вино́, пи́во, мо́рс, кисе́ль, кефи́р, компо́т, ква́с.
Napitki : vodá, cháj, kófe, vinó, pívo, mórs,kisel',kefir, kompót, kvás.
नापितकी – वदा, चाय, कोफे, विनो, पिवा, मोरस, कीसिल, कफिर, कमपोत, कवास।
Beverages: water, tea, coffee, wine, stewed cranberry drink, yogurt, compote, kvass.

Мя́со: говя́дина, свини́на, бара́нина, теля́тина.
Mjaso: govjadina, svinina, baranina, teljatina.
मयासा – गवयाजिना, सविनिना, बरानिना, चिलयाचिना।
Meat: beef, pork, lamb, veal.

Пти́ца: ку́рица, у́тка, гусь, фаза́н, инде́йка.
Ptitsa: kuritsa, utka, gus', fazan, indejka.
प्तचीत्सा – कूरीत्सा, उतका, गूस, फ़जान, इनजेयका।
Poultry: chicken, duck, goose, pheasant, turkey.

Жа́реный, печёный, варёный.
Zharenyj, pechjonyj, varjonyj.
जारेनी, पिछयोनी, वारयोनी।
Fried, baked, boiled.

CHAPTER

8 Tell us About Your Hobbies

Увлече́ние	Uvlechenie
hobby	उवलेछेनीय
Увлека́ться (чем?)	Uvlekat'sja (chem?)
to have a hobby, to be keen on smth.	उवलेकातस्या
Досу́г, на досу́ге	Dosug, na dosuge
leisure, at one's leisure	दसूग, नादासूगे
Проводи́ть досу́г	Provodit' dosug
to spend time	प्रवाजिच दसूग
Свобо́дное вре́мя	Svobodnoe vremja
spare time	स्वाबोदनय व्रेमिया
О́тдых, отдыха́ть	Otdykh, otdykhat'
rest, recreation; to have a rest	ओदिख, आदिखाच
Кани́кулы	Kanikuly
vacation	कानीकूली
О́тпуск	Otpusk
holiday	ओतपूस्क

DIALOGUE - 1

Чем ты занимáешься в свобóдное врéмя?

Chem ty zanimaesh'sja v svobodnoe vremja?

छेम ती जनीमायशस्या ब स्वबोदन्य व्रेमिया?

What do you do in your spare time?

В свобóдное врéмя я слýшаю мýзыку, читáю, хожý в спорти́вный зал, на дискотéку. А ты как провóдишь свóй досýг?

V svobodnoe vremja ja slushaju muzyku, chitaju, khozhu v sportivnyj zal, na diskoteku. A ty kak provodish' svoj dosug?

व स्वबोदन्य व्रमिया या स्लूशयू मूजिकू, छितायू, खज्झू व स्प्रचीवनी ज़ाल, ना दिस्काचेकू। आ ति काक प्रवोजिश स्वोई दसूक?

In my spare time I listen to music, read, go to the gym, to the disc. And how do you spend time?

Обы́чно я бывáю с друзья́ми и́ли дóма, и́ли за гóродом, на прирóде. Чáсто хóдим в бар.

Obychno ja byvaju s druz'jami ili doma, ili za gorodom, na prirode. Chasto khodim v bar.

अबिछना या बिवायू स द्रूजयामी ईली दोमा, ईली जा गोरदम, नाप्रिरोदे! छासता खजीम व बार।

Usually I am with friends or at home, or in the suburbs, outside. We often go to the bar.

DIALOGUE - 2

Ты люби́шь танцевáть?

Ty ljubish' tantsevat'?

ति लूबिश तनसेवाच?

Do you like to dance?

Обожа́ю. Я не то́лько быва́ю на диското́ках, но занима́юсь ещё в танцева́льной сту́дии.

Obozhaju. Ja ne tol'ko byvaju na diskotekakh, no zanimajus' eshhjo v tantseval'noj studii.

अबाज्झायू! या नि तोलका बिवायू ना दिसकाचेयकाक, इशो व तनसेवालनय स्तूजि।

I love it. I not only go to the discs, but I also go for dance classes.

А где така́я сту́дия нахо́дится?

A gde takaja studija nakhoditsja?

आ गिजे तकाया स्तूजीया नाखोदीतस्या?

And where is the dance studio?

В До́ме культу́ры. Я хожу́ туда́ три ра́за в неде́лю. Мы у́чимся танцева́ть совреме́нные и ру́сские наро́дные та́нцы, а та́кже та́нцы наро́дов ми́ра.

V Dome kul'tury. Ja khozhu tuda tri raza v nedelju. My uchimsja tantsevat' sovremennye i russkie narodnye tantsy, a takzhe tantsy narodov mira.

वदोमे कूलतूरी, या खजू तूदा त्री राज़ा वनिजेलयू! मी उछीमसीया तनसेवाच सवरेमेनिय ई रूसकीये नारोदनीय तानसी, आ ताकजे तानसी नारोदव मीरा!

In the cultural house. I go there thrice a week. We learn modern dance and Russian folk dances and dance from all over the world.

А ты увлекаешься чем-нибудь?

A ty uvlekaesh'sja chem-nibud'?

आ ती उवलेकायश्स्या छेमनिबूच?

Do you have a hobby?

Мои увлече́ния всё вре́мя меня́лись: увлека́лся тури́змом, та́нцами, пел, игра́л на гита́ре и да́же рисова́л. Занима́лся те́ннисом, фигу́рным ката́нием.

Moi uvlechenija vsyo vremja menjalis': uvlekalsja turizmom, tantsami, pel, igral na gitare i dazhe risoval. Zanimalsja tennisom, figurnym kataniem.

मई उवलेछेनिया व्स्यो व्रेमिया मिनयालिस—उवलेकालसया तूरीजमम, तानसामी, पेल, इगराल ना गितारे ई दाजे रिसावाल! जनीमालस्या तेनीसम, फिगूरनीम कतानियम।

My hobbies kept changing all the time: I was fascinated by tourism, dance, used to sing, played the guitar and even painted. I played tennis, did figure skating.

а) **много**

почти нет **У меня мало свободного времени**

нет

б) **— Как вы проводите свое свободное время?**

— Я занимаюсь спортом.

CHAPTER 9

Sport

Стадио́н	Stadión	स्तजियोन	Stadium
Спорти́вная/ Волейбо́льная/ Баскетбо́льная площа́дка	Sportívnaya/ Volyeyból'naya/ Baskyetból'naya ploshshádka	स्परचीवनया/ वलेबोलनया/ बस्केतबोलनया प्लशादका	Sports /Volleyball/ Basketball field
Те́ннисный ко́рт	Tyénnisniy kórt	चेनिसनी कोर्त	Tennis court
Спорти́вный, Гимнасти́ческий зал	Sportívniy, Gimnastíchyeskiy zal	स्परचीवनी, गिमनासतीछेसकी ज़ाल	Gymnasium
Бассе́йн	Bassyéyn	बसेन	Swimming pool
Като́к	Katók	कतोक	Skating-rink
Турни́р	Toornír	तूरनीर	Tournament
Чемпиона́т ми́ра, ...	Chyempionát míra	छिमप्यानात मीरा	World championship
Соревнова́ния (по + Дат.падеж)	Soryevnovániya	सरेवनावानीया	Competitions
Трениро́вка	Tryenirówka	त्रेनीरोवका	Training; coaching
Матч	Match	माच	Match

Чемпио́н, чемпио́нка	Chyempión, chyempiónka	छेमप्योन, छेमप्योनका	Champion
Ма́стер спо́рта (по + Дат. падеж)	Mástyer spórta	मास्त्येर स्पोर्ता	Master of sport(s)
Тре́нер	Tryényer	त्रेनिर	Coach
Выи́грывать/ вы́играть матч,	Viígrivat'/ víigrat' match	विग्रीवच/विग्रच माच	To win a match
Встре́чу (со счётом...)	Vstryéchoo (so schyotom...)	व्स्त्रेछू (स श्योतम)	A game (with a score of….)
Прои́грывать/проигра́ть	Proígrivat'/proigrát'	प्रइग्रीवच/प्रइग्राच	To lose
Победи́ть, Одержа́ть/ Оде́рживать побе́ду	Pobyedít', dyerzhát'/ Odyérzhivat' pobyédoo	पबेजीच, अदेरज्झाच/ अदेरज्झीवच पब्येदू	To win, to gain a victory over
Сыгра́ть вничью́, Со счётом	Sigrát' vnich'yoó, So schyotom	स्ग्राच वीनछ्यू, स श्योतम	To make a draw;
Заня́ть (завоева́ть)/ занима́ть	Zanyát' (zavoyevát')/ zanimát'	ज़न्याच (ज़वएवाच)/ज़नीमाच	To end the game with a score….
(Завое́вывать) пе́рвое ме́сто	(Zavoyévivat') pyérvoye myésto	(ज़वयेवीवाच) पेरवए मेस्ता	To gain first place
Боле́льщик,	Bolyél'shshik	बलेलशिक	Fan
Боле́ть (за + Вин. падеж)	Bolyét'	बल्येच	To be a fan

DIALOGUE 1

Ты занима́ешься спо́ртом?

Ty zanimaesh'sja sportom?

ती जनीमाएशस्या स्पोर्तम?

Do you play sports?

Да, занима́юсь.

Da, zanimajus'

दा जनीमायुस।

Yes I do play.

Каки́ми вида́ми?

Kakimi vidami?

ककीमी विदामी?

What kinds of sports?

Зимо́й я хожу́ на лы́жах, ле́том ката́юсь на велосипе́де и кру́глый год пла́ваю.

Zimoj ja khozhu na lyzhakh, letom katajus' na velosipede i kruglyj god plavaju.

जिमोई या खाजू ना लिजाख, लियतम कतायूस ना वेलीसीपेजे ई क्रूगली गौत पलावयु।

In winters I ski, in summers I ride the bicycle and I swim throughout the year.

И у тебя́ на всё хвата́ет вре́мени?

I u tebja na vsyo khvataet vremeni?

ई उचीबिया ना व्स्यो खवातायत व्रेमेनी?

And you manage to take out time for everything?

Не всегда́. Ведь я учу́сь в университе́те. В бассе́йн я хожу́ два ра́за в неде́лю, по у́трам. На лы́жах ката́юсь то́лько по воскресе́ньям.

Ne vsegda. Ved' ja uchus' v universitete. V bassejn ja khozhu dva raza v nedelju, po utram.Na lyzhakh katajus' tol'ko po voskresen'jam.

नी सिगदा! वेज या उछूस व उनीवेरसीचेचे! व बासेन या खजू-दवा राजा निजेलेयू, प उत्राम! ना लिज़ाख कतायूस तोलका प वसक्रेसेनियाम।

Not always. Since I study in the university. I go to the swimming pool twice a week, in the mornings. I ski only on Sundays.

Давно́ ты занима́ешься спо́ртом?

Davno ty zanimaesh'sja sportom?

दावनो ति जनीमायशस्या स्पोरतम?

Are you playing sports from a long time?

Давно́, с де́тства.

Davno, s detstva.

दवनो स जियतस्तवा।

Yes, since childhood.

DIALOGUE - 2

Приве́т! Ты на стадио́н?

Privet! Ty na stadion?

प्रिवियत! ती ना स्तजीयोन?

Hi! Are you at the stadium?

Да, сего́дня "Дели Даэрдевилс" игра́ет со "Ченнай Суперкингсом".

Da, segodnja "Deli Dajerdevils" igraet so "Chennaj Superkingsom".

दा सिवोदनिया "डैली डेयर डेव्वलस" इगरायत स "चेनईसपुरग्स्मि"।

Yes today "Delhi Daredevils" is playing against :Chennai Superkings".

Ты был на про́шлом ма́тче?

Ty byl na proshlom matche?

ती बिल ना प्रोशलम माचे?

Did you go for the last match?

Да. Тогда́ соревнова́ния зако́нчились побе́дой "ККР".

Da. Togda sorevnovanija zakonchilis' pobedoj "KKR".

दा! तगदा सरेवनावानिया जाकोनाछिलीस पाबेदई के.के.आर।

Yes. That time KKR had won.

А я ду́мал, что вы́играл "Дели Даэрдевилс".

A ja dumal, chto vyigral "Deli Dajerdevils".

दा या दूमल श्तो विगरल डेलीडेयर डेव्वलस।

But, I thought "Delhi Daredevils" had won.

Нет, я по́мню то́чно, счёт был 2 : 1 (два один).

Net, ja pomnju tochno, schjot byl 2 : 1 (dva odin).

नियत या पोमनियो तोछना शियोत बिल 2 : 1

No, I remember the score was 2 : 1.

CHAPTER

10 Travel

Choosing an itinerary

Маршру́т	Marshroót	मर्शरूत	Route, itinerary
Выбира́ть/ вы́брать маршру́т	Vibirát'/víbrat' marshroót	विबीराच/वीबरच मर्शरूत	To choose an itinerary
Поездка́ (по стране́, за грани́цу, в Москву́...)	Poyezdka (po stranye, za granitsoo, v Moskvoo...)	पयेज़्दका (प स्त्राने, ज़ा ग्रानीत्सू, व म्सक्वू)	Trip (round the country, abroad, to Moscow)
Путеше́ствие (по стране́, за грани́цей)	Pootyeshyéstviye (po stranyé, za granítsyey)	पूचेशेस्तविये (प स्त्राने, ज़ा ग्रानीत्सू)	Journey, trip
Соверши́ть путеше́ствие/ Путеше́ствовать	Sovyershít' pootyeshyéstviye/ Pootyeshyéstvovat'	सवेरशीच पूचेशेस्तविये/ पूचेशेस्तवोवच	To journey, to travel
Круи́з по Средизе́мному морю́,	Krooíz po Sryedizyémnomoo moryoó,	क्रूइज़ प स्रीजीज़िमनोमो र्मयू	Cruise round the Mediterranean sea
Тур, Шо́п-тур по Ита́лии, ...	Toor, Shóp-tur po Itálii	तूर, शोपतूर प इताली	Tour, shop tour around Italy,....
Тури́ст	Turíst	तूरीस्त	Tourist

DIALOGUE - 1

Здра́вствуйте! Туристи́ческое аге́нтство "СОТС" слу́шает.
Zdravstvujte! Turisticheskoe agentstvo "SOTC" slu-shaet.
जद्रास्तूईचे! तूरीसतीछस्कए आगेनसत्वा ऐसोटीसी-सलूशयत।
Hello! This is the travel agency "SOTC"

Скажи́те, пожа́луйста, каки́е пое́здки вы мо́жете предложить?
Skazhite, pozhalujsta, kakie poezdki vy mozhete predlozhit'?
सकाजिचे पजालूसता काकिये पायेजदकी वी मोजिचे प्रिदलाजिच?
Can you please recommend me some tours?

Круи́зы, шо́п-ту́ры, экскурсио́нные и авто́бусные ту́ры, авиабиле́ты во все страны́ ми́ра. Что вас конкре́тно интересу́ет?
Kruizy, shop-tury, jekskursionnye i avtobusnye tury, aviabilety vo vse strany mira. Chto vas konkretno interesuet?
क्रूयूजी, शोपतूरी, एक्सकूरसीयोनीये ई अफतोबूसनीये तूरी, अवयाबिलयेती व व्स्ये स्त्रानी मीरा! श्तो वास-कनक्रेयतना इंचेरेसूयत?
Cruises, shop tours, excursions and bus tours, air ticket booking. What exactly are you interested in?

Я хотел бы побывать на курорте.
Ja khotel by pobyvat' na kurorte.
या खाचेल बी पबीवाच न कूरोरच्चे।
I would like to go to a resort.

У нас есть путёвки на таки́е куро́рты в Слова́кию — от 245 до́лларов, А́встрию — от 460 до́лларов, Фра́нцию - от 690 до́лларов.

U nas est' putjovki na takie kurorty v Slovakiju — ot 245 dollarov, Avstriju — ot 460 dollarov, Franciju - ot 690 dollarov.

उनास यस्त पूचयोवकी ना ताकीये कूरोरती व स्लवाकियू-अत 245, आफस्त्रीयू-अत 460, फ्रांसीयू-अत 690।

We have tours for resorts in Slovakia- 245 $ onwards, to Austria – 460 $ onwards, France- 690 $ onwards.

Дорогова́то.

Dorogovato.

दरगावाता।

It's expensive.

Вы мо́жете съе́здить на инди́йские куро́рты, наприме́р, в "Го́а", там отли́чные пляжи, цена путёвки 500 рубле́й.

Vy mozhete sjezdit' na indijskie kurorty, naprimer, v "Goa", tam otlichnye pljazhi, tsena putjovki 500 rublej.

वी मोजिचे स्येजिच ना इनजिसकीय कूरोरती नाप्रिमयर व गोवा, ताम अतलिछनीय प्लयाजी, त्सिना पूचयोवकी 500 रूबलेई।

You can go to Indian resorts, to "Goa", they have excellent beaches there, and the tour would cost 500 rubles.

Хорошо́. Спаси́бо за информа́цию. Я поду́маю над ва́шим предложе́нием.

Khorosho. Spasibo za informatsiju. Ja podumaju nad vashim predlozheniem.

खराशो! प्सीबा जा इनफरमातस्यू! या पादूमयू नाद वाशीम प्रिदलाजेनियम।

O.K. Thank you for the information. I will think it over.

DIALOGUE - 2

Я слышал, вы собира́етесь в путеше́ствие по “Золото́му кольцу́”?

Ja slyshal, vy sobiraetes' v puteshestvie po “Zolotomu kol'tsu”?

या सलीशल वी सबीरायचेस व पूचेशेतवीय प जलातोमू कलत्सू?

I came to know that you are planning to travel around the “Golden Ring of Russia”?

Да, мы там ни разу не были, но мно́го слы́шали о нём.

Da, my tam ni razu ne byli, no mnogo slyshali o njom.

दा मी ताम नी राजू नी बिली, नो मनोगा स्लीशली अ नियोम।

Yes, we haven't been there even once, but have heard a lot about it.

Там есть мно́го посмотре́ть. Ведь этот маршру́т прохо́дит по дре́вним русским города́м, в кото́рых сохрани́лись архитекту́рные памятники и древняя живопись.

Tam est' chto posmotret'. Ved' jetot marshrut prokhodit po drevnim russkim gorodam, v kotorykh sokhranilis' arhitekturnye pamjatniki i drevnjaja zhivopis'.

ताम यस्त श्तो पसमातरेच। वियेच एतत मारशरूत प्राखोजित प दरेवनीय रूसकीम गरादाम व कतोरीख सखरालिनीस अरखीतूरनीये पामितनिकी ई द्रेवनया जिवापीस।

There is lots to see, as the route goes through the ancient Russian towns, where there are landmarks and ancient paintings.

А ско́лько таки́х городо́в?

A skol'ko takikh gorodov?

आ सकोलका ताकिख गारादोव?

And how many such cities are there?

Е́сли я не ошиба́юсь, — семь: Росто́в, Заго́рск, Переяславль-Залесский, Влади́мир, Су́здаль, Яросла́вль, Кострома́.

Esli ja ne oshibajus', — sem': Rostov, Zagorsk, Perejaslavl'-Zalesskij, Vladimir, Suzdal', Jaroslavl', Kostroma.

येसली या नी अशीबायुस-सेम-रसतोव, जागोरस्क, पेरेयासलावल-जालेयसकी-वलदीमीर, सूजदल, योरोसलाविल, कसतोरमा।

If I am not mistaken, then there are seven: Rostov, Zagorsk, pereyaslavl- Zalesskii, Vladimir, Suzdal, Yaroslavl, and Kostroma.

Нам сказа́ли, что мы мо́жем познако́миться со ста́рыми ру́сскими промы́слами.

Nam skazali, chto my mozhem poznakomit'sja so starymi russkimi promyslami.

नाम सकाजालि श्तो मी मोजिम पजनाकोमितस्या स स्तारीमी रूसकीमी प्रमीस्लामी।

We were told, that we can see Old Russian handicraft.

Да, там спло́шь и ря́дом прода́ются деревя́нные и гли́няные игру́шки.

Da, tam splosh' i rjadom prodajutsja derevjannye i glinjanye igrushki.

दा ताम स्पोलश इ रियादम प्रदायुत्या जेरेवयानिये ई गलीयानिये इगरूशकी।

Yes, over there wooden and clay toys are sold everywhere.

Одни́м сло́вом, лу́чше оди́н раз уви́деть, чем сто раз услы́шать.

Odnim slovom, luchshe odin raz uvidet', chem sto raz uslyshat'.

अदनीम सलोवम लूशेय अजीन रास उवीजेच छेम स्तो रास उसलीशच।

In one word, seeing is believing.

CHAPTER

11 Journey by Train

Ка́сса(-ы) железнодоро́жного вокза́ла
Kassa(-y) zheleznodorozhnogo vokzala
कासा (ई) जिलेजना दाराजनवा वकजाला
Booking- office

Расписа́ние поездо́в
Raspisanie poezdov
रसपिसानिये पयजदोव
Train schedule

Куда?	Where to?
kuda?	कुदा
в Москву	to Moscow
V Moskvu	व मस्कवू
до Москвы	till Moscow
Do Moskvy	द मसक्वी
На какое число?	On which date?
na kakoe chislo?	न काकोई छिसलो
на сегодня,	for today
na segodnja	न सिवोदनिया, न जाफतरा
на завтра	for tomorrow
na zavtra	ना स्रेदू, छितवर्यक
Биле́т Bilet Ticket На по́езд Волгогра́д—Москва́ на 8-е ма́я	For the train from Volgograd to Moscow on the 8th of May.

na poezd Volgograd—Moskva na 8- e maja	ना पोयजद वोलगाग्राद — मसकवा ना वसमोए माया
На рейс 311: Волгогра́д—Москва́	Train number 311: Volgograd- Moscow
na rejs 311: Volgograd—Moskva	ना रेस 311 — वोलगाग्राद — मस्क्वाा
в мя́гкий ваго́н	in a first-class coach,
v mjagkij vagon	व मयाकी वागोन
на фи́рменный по́езд	in a deluxe train
na firmennyj poezd	न फीरमीनी पोयजद
биле́т в купе́йный ваго́н	in a sleeping car
Bilet v kupejnyj vagon	बिलियत व कूपेनी वागोन
на ско́рый по́езд	in an express train
na skoryj poezd	न सकोरी पोयजद
в о́бщий ваго́н	in a general coach,
V obshhij vagon	व ओबशी वागोन
на пассажи́рский по́езд	in a slow passenger train.
na passazhirskij poezd	ना पसााजिरसकी पोयजद

DIALOGUE - 1

Скажи́те, пожа́луйста, у вас есть биле́ты в Москву́?
Skazhite, pozhalujsta, u vas est' bilety v Moskvu?
स्काजिचे पजालूसता उवास यस्त् बिलयति व मस्क्वू?
Excuse me; do you have tickets for Moscow?

Да. На како́й по́езд вы хоти́те купи́ть биле́т?
Da. Na kakoj poezd vy khotite kupit' bilet?
दा! ना काकोए पोयजद वी खाचीचे कूपिच बिलयत?
Yes, you want a ticket for which train?

На по́езд № 1 (но́мер оди́н). Он прихо́дит в Москву́ у́тром в 10.26 (десять двадцать шесть)?

Na poezd № 1(nomer odin). On prikhodit v Moskvu utrom v 10.26 (dyesyat' dvadtsat' shyest')?

ना पोयजद नोमर अजीन! ओन प्रिखोजित व मस्क्वू उतरम व 10.26?

For train No. 1. It reaches Moscow at 10:26 a.m.

Да, но на этот по́езд у́же нет биле́тов.

Da, no na jetot poezd uzhe net biletov.

दा नो ना एतत पोयजद उज्झे नियत बिलयतव।

But, there are no tickets for this train.

О́чень жаль! А что же мне де́лать? Это о́чень удо́бный по́езд: ложи́шься спать в Волгограде, а у́тром — уже в Москве́.

Ochen' zhal'! A chto zhe mne delat'? Jeto ochen' udobnyj poezd: lozhish'sja spat' v Volgograde, a utrom — uzhe v Moskve.

ओछिन ज्झाल! आ श्तो जय मिनिये जेलच! एता ओछीन उदोबनी पोयजद–लजिशस्या स्पात्च व वोलगाग्राजे, आ उतरम–उजै व मसक्वीये।

That's sad! Now, what should I do? It's a very comfortable train: one can lie down to sleep in Volgograd and in the morning reach Moscow.

Посмотри́те расписа́ние поездо́в: 15 (пятна́дцатый) то́же мо́жно назва́ть ночны́м по́ездом.

Posmotrite raspisanie poezdov: 15 (pjatnadtsatyj) tozhe mozhno nazvat' nochnym poezdom.

पसमात्रीचे रसपिसानिये पयेज़दोफ: 15–पितनादस्ती तोजे मोजना नजवाच नछनीम पोयजदम।

Please see the train schedule: train No. 15 is also a night train.

Спаси́бо, я поду́маю.

Spasibo, ja podumaju.

स्पसीबा या पदूमयू।

Thank you, I will think over.

DIALOGUE - 2

Скажи́те, а как хо́дят пое́зда на Москву́?

Skazhite, a kak khodjat poezda na Moskvu?

स्काज़ीचे आ काक खाजयात पयजदा ना मसक्वू?

Please tell me what is the schedule of trains to Moscow?

Ежедне́вно два пое́зда, о́ба ско́рые, и че́рез день — 2 (два) пассажирских.

Ezhednevno dva poezda, oba skorye, i cherez den' — 2 (dva) passazhirskikh

यजेदनेवना दावा पयजदा, ओबा सकोरिये ई छिरज जेन–दवा पसाजिरसिकिक।

Everyday there are two trains, both are express trains, on alternate days there are 2 slow passenger trains.

Прости́те, а кака́я ра́зница?

Prostite, a kakaja raznitsa?

प्रसचिचे आ काकाया राज़नितसा?

Excuse me, but what is the difference?

Ско́рый идёт до Москвы́ 18 (восемна́дцать) часо́в, пассажи́рский почти́ су́тки, 22 (два́дцать два) часа́.

Skoryj idjot do Moskvy 18 (vosyemnádtsat') chasov, passazhirskij pochti sutki, 22 (dvádtsat' dva)chasa

स्कोरी इजयोत द मसक्वी 18 छिसोव, पशाजिरीरीसकि पाचती सूतकी, 22 छिसा

The express train reaches Moscow in 18 hours, and the slow passenger train takes almost a day, 22 hours.

А когда́ отправля́ются ско́рые?

A kogda otpravljajutsja skorye?

आ कगदा अतप्रावलयायूतस्या स्कोरिये?

And when do the express trains leave?

В 14.30 (четы́рнадцать, три́дцать) и 18.08 (восемна́дцать, во́семь).

V 14.30 (chyetírnadtsat' trídtsat') i 18.08 (vosyemnádtsat' vósyem').

व (छितिरनादत्सच त्रिदत्सच) इ (वसिमनादत्सच वोसिम).

At 14.30 hours and 18.08 hours.

Да́йте мне, пожа́луйста, два биле́та на тот, кото́рый ухо́дит в 14.30 (четы́рнадцать, три́дцать).

Dajte mne, pozhalujsta, dva bileta na tot, kotoryj ukhodit v 14.30 (chyetírnadtsat', trídtsat').

दाईचे मिनिये पजालूसता दवा बिलयता ना तोत कातोरी उखोजित व 14.30।

Please give me two tickets for the train which leaves at 14.30 hours.

В како́м ваго́не: купе́йном, плацка́ртном ?

V kakom vagone: kupejnom, plats-kartnom ?

व काकोम वागोने—कूपेनम, प्लात्सकारतनम?

In which compartment: in a sleeping car or in a carriage with numbered reserved seats?

В купе́йном ; да́йте, пожа́луйста, одно́ ве́рхнее ме́сто, а друго́е — ни́жнее.

V kupejnom ; dajte, pozhalujsta, odno verhnee mesto, a drugoe — nizhnee.

व कूपेनम—दाईचे पजालूसता अदनो वेयरखनीय म्यस्ता, आ द्रुगोई निजनये।

In a sleeping car please. One upper birth and the other lower birth.

CHAPTER

12 Travelling by Air

Рейс(-ы) на Москву́, на Волгогра́д...	Flight to Moscow, to Volgograd
Ryeys(-i) na Moskvoo, na Volgograd...	रेस(इ) ना मस्कवु, ना वल्गाग्राद....
Вы́лет рейса (самолёта)	Departure of a plane
Vílyet ryeysa (samolyota)	विलयत रेसा (समाल्योता)
Регистра́ция (биле́тов и бага́жа) на рейс 302, ...	Registration (of tickets and baggage) for flight 302,
Ryegistrátsiya (bilyétov i bagázha) na ryeys 302, ...	रेगिसस्त्रात्स्या (बिलयेतव इ बगाज्झा) ना रेस 302...
Регистри́ровать/ зарегистри́ровать биле́т	To register a ticket
Ryegistrirovat'/ zaryegistrirovat' bilyet	रेगिसत्रिरोवच/जारेगिसत्रिरोवच बिलयेत
Сто́йка регистра́ции	Registration desk
Stóyka ryegistrátsii	स्तोइका रेगिसस्त्रात्सि
Поса́дка (пассажи́ров, самолёта)	Boarding; landing
Posádka (passazhírov, samolyota)	पसादका (पसाज़िरफ, समाल्योता)
Соверша́ть/соверши́ть Поса́дку	To make a landing
Sovyershát'/sovyershít' Posádkoo	सवेरशाच/सवेरशीच पसादकू

Заде́ржка рейса (поса́дки на самолёт)	Delay of a flight, of a boarding
Zadyérzhka ryeysa (posádki na samolyot)	ज़ार्देज्झक़ा रेसा (पसादकी ना समाल्योत)
Заде́рживаться/задержа́ться	To delay
Zadyérzhivat'sya/zadyerzhát'sya	ज़ार्देज्झीवत्स्या/ ज़ार्देज्झात्स्या
Трап	Ladder
Trap	त्राप
Иллюмина́тор	Porthole, sidelight
Illyoominátor	इल्युमीनातर
Полёт(-ы)	Flight(s)
Polyot(-i)	पल्योत(इ)
Бортпрово́дник(-ница)	Air steward
Bortprovódnik(-nitsa)	बोर्तप्रवोदनिक (नित्सा)
Стюарде́сса	Stewardess
Styooardyéssa	स्तूअरदेसा
Приземля́ться/ Приземли́ться	To land
Prizyemlyat'sya/ Prizyemlit'sya	प्रिजिमल्यात्स्या/प्रिजिमलित्स्या

DIALOGUE - 1

Ска́жите, пожа́луйста, когда́ начина́ется поса́дка на рейс 302 (три́ста два)?

Skazhite, pozhalujsta, kogda nachinaetsja posadka na rejs 302 (trista dva)?

शकाजिचे पजालूसता कगदा नछीनायतस्या पसादका ना रेस 302?

Please tell me when does the boarding for flight No. 302 start?

Мне ка́жется, объяви́ли заде́ржку э́того рейса. Спроси́те в спра́вочном бюро́.

Mne kazhetsja, objjavili zaderzhku jetogo rejsa. Sprosite v spravochnom bjuro.

मिनीये काजीतस्या, अबेविलि जादेरजकू एतवा रेसा! स्प्रसीचे व स्प्रावछनम बियूरो।

I think it has been announced that the flight is delayed. Please inquire from the information bureau.

Извини́те, вы не ска́жете, на ско́лько заде́рживается рейс 302 (три́ста два)?

Izvinite, vy ne skazhete, na skol'ko zaderzhivaetsja rejs 302 (trista dva)?

इजवनीचे वी नी स्काजीचे ना स्कोलका जादेरजीवायतस्या रेस 302?

Excuse me, could you please tell me by how many hours is the flight No.302 delayed?

Он лети́т по расписа́нию.

On letit po raspisaniju.

ओन लिचित प रसपिसानियू।

It is flying according to schedule.

Извини́те, у како́й сто́йки бу́дет регистра́ция биле́тов и бага́жа на этот рейс?

Izvinite, u kakoj stojki budet registracija biletov i bagazha na jetot rejs?

इज विनीचे उ काकोई स्तोईकी बूजित रेगिस्त्रात्सिया बिल्यितफ ई बगाजा ना एतत रेस?

Excuse me, at which registration desk will the registration for tickets and baggage take place for this flight?

Регистра́ция у́же начала́сь у сто́йки № 2 (но́мер два).

Registracija uzhe nachalas' u stojki № 2 (nomer dva).

रेगिस्त्रात्सया उजै नछालस उ सतोईकी नोमेर दवा।

The registration has already started at desk No.2.

А где вы́ход на поса́дку?

A gde vykhod na posadku?

आ गिजे विखद ना पसादकू?

And where is the departure gate?

Вы́ход № 1 (но́мер оди́н).
Vykhod № 1 (nomer odin).
विखद नोमिर अजीन।
Gate No.1

Спаси́бо.
Spasibo.
स्पसीबा।
Thank you.

Не опаздывайте! Счастли́вого полёта!
Ne opazdyvajte! Schastlivogo poljota!
नी अपाजदीवयचे! शयसलिववा पालोयता!
Don't get late! Have a safe flight!

DIALOGUE - 2

Ска́жите, пожа́луйста, где моё ме́сто?
Skazhite, pozhalujsta, gde mojo mesto?
शाकाजिचे पजालूसता गिजिय मयो मियस्ता?
Please tell me, where is my seat?
Разреши́те ваш биле́т! Пятна́дцатое "Г". Второ́й сало́н, нале́во.
Razreshite vash bilet! Pjatnadtsatoe "G". Vtoroj salon, nalevo.
रजारीशिचे वाश बिलियेत! पितनातसतये "B"! व्तोरोई सालोन, नलेयवा।
Kindly show your ticket! Fifteenth row "C". Second cabin on the left.

А в пе́рвом сало́не мест нет?
A v pervom salone mest net?
आ व पेरवम सालोने मेस्त नियत?
Are there seats in the first cabin?

Подождите, пока все пассажиры сядут. Я посмотрю.
Podozhdite, poka vse passazhiry sjadut. Ja posmotrju.
पदाजिचे, पका व्से पसाजिरी स्यादूत। या पसमात्रयू!
Please wait! Let all the passengers take their seat. Let me check.

Спасибо. Мы прилетаем в четырнадцать тридцать?
Spasibo. My priletaem v chetyrnadtsat' tridtsat'?
स्पासीबा। मी प्रिलितायम व छिर्तानातसज त्रिदसज?
Thank you we will be flying at 2:30 p.m.

Да. В Дели. А сейчас, пожалуйста, сядьте на своё место.
Da. V Deli. A sejchas, pozhalujsta, sjad'te na svojo mesto.
दा व देली! आ छियास पजालूसता स्याचे ना सवयो मियस्ता।
Yes, to Delhi. Now, kindly be seated.

Пассажир, проснитесь! Вы будете обедать?
Passazhir, prosnites'! Vy budete obedat'?
पसाजिर प्रसनिचेस! वि बूजीचे अबयेदच?
Please wake up! Will you have lunch?

А... обедать? Да, буду.
A... obedat'? Da, budu.
आ अबयेदच! दा बूदू।
Lunch? Yes, I will.

Из напитков есть кофе, чай, минеральная вода. Что вы желаете?
Iz napitkov est' kofe, chaj, mineral'naja voda. Chto vy zhelaete?
इज नापितकफ यस्त कोफ, चाय, मिनरालनया वदा! श्तो वी जेलाइचे?
For beverages we have coffee, tea and mineral water. What would you like?

Ко́фе, пожа́луйста.
Kofe, pozhalujsta.
कोफे पजालूसता।
Coffee please.

Сейча́с принесу́. Хоти́те журна́лы, газе́ты?
Sejchas prinesu. Khotite zhurnaly, gazety?
शीछ्यास प्रिनेसू! खाचीचे जूरनाली, गाजेयती?
I will just get it. Would you like magazines or newspapers?

Да, принеси́те, пожа́луйста.
Da, prinesite, pozhalujsta.
दा प्रिनीसीचे पजालूसता।
Yes please.

Пассажи́р, вам что, пло́хо?
Passazhir, vam chto, plokho?
प्रशाजीर वाम श्तो, पलोखा?
Are you alright?

Да, меня́ немно́го укача́ло.
Da, menja nemnogo ukachalo.
दा मिनिया निमनोगा उकाछला।
I am slightly airsick.

Я сейча́с принесу́ вам минера́льной воды́.
Ja sejchas prinesu vam mineral'noj vody.
या शिछ्यास प्रिनेसू वाम मिनरालनेय वदि।
I will just get you some mineral water.

Вы́пейте пожа́луйста.
Vypejte pozhalujsta.
विपिचे पजालूसता।
Please drink.

Спаси́бо.
Spasibo.
स्पस्बिा।
Thank you.

Вот вам журна́лы, почита́йте.
Vot vam zhurnaly, pochitajte.
वोत वाम जूरनाली, पछितायचे।
Here are some magazines for you.

Спаси́бо ещё раз, огро́мное!
Spasibo eshhjo raz, ogromnoe!
स्पसीबा ईशो रास अगरोमने!
Thank you very much!

False Friends of a Translator: are pairs of words in two languages that appear to be similar, but differ in meaning. For example:

1.	Администра́ция	Management, Authorities
2.	Аккура́тный	Neat, Tidy
3.	Акту́альный	Important, Relevant
4.	Аргуме́нт	Reason/ Reasoning, Point
5.	База́р	Market, Market Place
6.	Балл	Marks, Point, Number, Grades
7.	Балло́н	Cylinder, Can
8.	Бензи́н	Gasoline
9.	Бриллиа́нт	Diamond
10.	Ваго́н	Car, Carriage

11.	Газе́та	Newspaper
12.	Да́та	Date
13.	Дива́н	Sofa
14.	Журна́л	Magazine
15.	Исто́рия	History
16.	Кабине́т	Study, Office, Consulting Room
17.	Ка́мера	Prison Cell
18.	Кампа́ния	Campaign
19.	Класс	Classroom
20.	Кома́нда	Team
21.	Компа́ния	Company
22.	Костю́м	Suit
23.	Магази́н	Shop
24.	Маши́на	Car
25.	Ми́тинг	Rally, Mass Public Demonstration
26.	Норма́льно	Well, Properly, O.K
27.	Проду́кт	Food
28.	Фа́брика	Factory, Plant
29.	Фами́лия	Surname
30.	Фи́зик	Physicist
31.	Шеф	Boss,Head, Chief, Leader

I Glossary

FEELINGS

Happy	Счастли́вый	Schastlivyj	शासलीवी
Thoughtful	Заду́мчивый	Zadumchivyj	जादूमछिवी
Thirsty	Испы́тывающий Жа́жду	Ispytyvajushhij Zhazhdu	इसपितीवयूशी ज़ाजदू
Sad	Гру́стный	Grustnyj	ग्रुसनी
Hungry	Голо́дный	Golodnyj	गालोदनी
Full	Наевшийся До́сыта	Naevshijsja Dosyta	नयेवछिसया दसीता
Ill	Больно́й	Bol'noj	बलनोइ
Well	Здоро́вый	Zdorovyj	जदारोवी
Shy	Засте́нчивый	Zastenchivyj	जसचेनछिवी
Angry	Серди́тый	Serdityj	सिरजीती
Sorry	Огорчённый	Ogorchjonnyj	अगरछयोनी
Sleepy	Со́нный	Sonnyj	सोननी
Hot	Жа́ркий	Zharkij	जारकी
Energetic	Энерги́чный	Jenergichnyj	एनेरगिछनी
Cold	Холо́дный	Holodnyj	खालोदनी
Bored	Ску́чный	Skuchnyj	स्कूछनी
Glad	Ра́достный	radostnyj	रादस्तनी

Professions

Teacher	Учи́тель	Uchítel’	उछीचल
House Painter	Маля́р	Maljár	मलयार
Singer	Певе́ц	Pevéts	पिवेयत्स
Pianist	Пиани́ст	Pianíst	पियानिस्त
Fireman	Пожа́рник	Pozhárnik	पजारनिक
Gardener	Садо́вник	Sadóvnik	सादोवनिक
Dentist	Зубно́й Вра́ч	Zubnój Vrách	जुबनोऐ व्राच
Doctor	Вра́ч	Vrách	व्राच
Ballet Dancer	Балери́на	Balerína	बलेरीना
Bus Driver	Води́тель Авто́буса	Vodítel’ Avtóbusa	वजीचेल अफतोबूसा
Hairdresser	Парикма́хер	Parikmákher	परीमाखिर
Judge	Судья́	Sud’já	सुजया
Mailman	Почтальо́н	Pochtal’ón	पछतालियोन
Air Hostess	Стюарде́сса	Stjuardéssa	स्तूआरदेसा
Pilot	Пило́т	Pilót	पिलोत
News Reader	Телекоммента́тор	Telekommentátor	चेलेकामिनतातिर
Astronaut	Астрона́вт	Astronávt	

Professor	Профе́ссор	Proféssor	प्राफेसर
Photographer	Фото́граф	Fotógraf	फताग्राफ
Policeman	Полице́йский	Politséjskij	पलीसियत्स्की
Mountaineer	Альпини́ст	Al’piníst	अलपीनिस्त
Sailor	Моря́к	Morják	मरयाक
Mechanic	Меха́ник	Mekhánik	मैखानिक
Author	Писа́тель	Pisátel’	पिसाचिल
Designer	Диза́йнер	Dizájner	दिजाईनर
Model	Манеке́нщица	Manekénshhitsa	मनेकेनशित्सा
Artist	Худо́жник	Khudózhnik	खुदोजनीक
Sculptor	Ску́льптор	Skúl’ptor	स्कुल्पतर
Cook	По́вар	Póvar	पोवर
Farmer	Фе́рмер	Férmer	फेरमर
Shopkeeper	Владе́лец Магази́на	Vladélets Magazína	वलाजेयत्स मगाज़िना

Cooking And Baking

Vinegar	У́ксус	Úksus	उकसूस
Rack	По́лка	Pólka	पोलका

Blender	Смеси́тель	Smesítel’	समेसिचल
Stove	Плита́	Plitá	प्लिता
Saucepan	Кастрю́ля	Kastrjúlja	कसत्रूलिया
Soup Pot	Супова́я Кастрю́ля	Supovája Kastrjúlja	सूपावया कसत्रूलिया
Saltshaker	Соло́нка	Solónka	सालोनका
Ladle	Поло́вник	Polóvnik	पलोविनक
Faucet	Кра́н	Krán	क्रान
Sink	Ра́ковина	Rákovina	राकाविना
Oil	Ма́сло	Máslo	मासला
Fish	Ры́ба	Rýba	रीबा
Platter	Блю́до	Bljúdo	बलूदा
Oven	Духо́вка	Dukhóvka	दूखोवका
Potato	Карто́фель, Карто́шка	Kartófel’, Kartóshka	करतोफिल, करतोषका
Duster	Тря́пка	Trjápka	त्रियपका
Apron	Фа́ртук	Fártuk	फारतुक
Mixingbowl	Ми́ска Для Сме́шивания	Míska Dlja Sméshivanija	मीसका, दल्या समेशीवनिया
Washing Machine	Стира́льная Маши́на	Stirál’naja Mashína	स्तीरालनया मशीना
Can Opener	Консе́рвный Но́ж	Konsérvnyj Nózh	कनसेरवनी नोश

Kettle	Ча́йник	Chájnik	छायनिक
Scale	Весы́	Vesý	वेयसी
Coffeepot	Кофе́йник	Koféjnik	काफैनिक
Utensil	Посу́да	Posúda	पसुदा
Refrigerator	Холоди́льник	Kholodíl'nik	खलाजिलनिक
Meat	Мя́со	Mjáso	मयासा
Egg Beater	Ве́нчик	Vénchik	वैनछिक
Doormat	Ко́врик	Kóvrik	कोवरिक
Colander	Дуршла́г	Durshlág	दुरषलाग
Gelatin	Желе́	Zhelé	जेले
Pepper Mill	Ме́льница Для Пе́рца	Mél'nitsa Dlja Pértsa	मेलनित्सा दल्या पेरत्सा
Table	Сто́л	Stól	सतोल
Cookbook	Пове́ренная Кни́га	Povérennaja Kníga	पोवरनया क्नीगा

AT THE MARKET

Vegetable Counter	Овощно́й Прила́вок	Ovoshhnój Prilávok	अवाशनोई प्रिलावक
Cucumber	Огуре́ц	Ogueréts	अगूरियत्स
Customer	Покупа́тель	Pokupátel'	पकूपाचिल

Grocer	Торго́вец	Torgóvets	तरगावियत्स
Tomato	Помидо́р	Pomidór	पमीदोर
Lettuce Салат	Лату́к	Latúk	लातूक
Onion	Лу́к	Lúk	लूक
Lemon	Лимо́н	Limón	लिमोन
Watermelon	Арбу́з	Arbúz	अरबूज
Cabbage	Капу́ста	Kapústa	कपूसता
Carrot	Морко́вь	Morkóv'	मरकोव
Cauliflower	Цветна́я Капу́ста	Tsvetnája Kapústa	स्वीतनाया कपूसता
Green Beans	Фасо́ль	Fasól'	फासोल
Capsicum	Пе́рец	Pérets	पैयरेत्स
Eggplant	Баклажа́н	Baklazhán	बकलाजान
Fruit Counter	Фрукто́вый Прила́вок	Fruktóvyj Prilávok	फ्रूकतोवी प्रिलावक
Banana	Бана́н	Banán	बनान
Orange	Апельси́н	Apel'sín	अपिलसीन
Grapes	Виногра́д	Vinográd	विनाग्राद
Pear	Гру́ша	Grúsha	ग्रुशा
Peach	Пе́рсик	Pérsik	पेरसीक

Melon	Ды́ня	Dýnja	दीनया
Pineapple	Анана́с	Ananás	अनानास
Gooseberry	Крыжо́вник	Kryzhóvnik	क्रीजोवनिक
Pomegranate	Грана́т	Granát	ग्रनात
Rasberries	Мали́на	Malína	मलीना
Strawberries	Клубни́ка	Klubníka	क्लुबनिका
Apple	Я́блока	Jábloka	याबलका
Egg	Яйцо́	Jajtsó	यत्सो
Bread	Хле́б	Khléb	खलेब
Tea	Ча́й	Cháj	चाय
Flour	Му́ка	Múka	मूका
Jam	Дже́м, Варе́нье	Dzhém, Varén'e	जैम, वारेनिय
Honey	Мёд	Mjod	मियोद
Shrimp	Креве́тка	Krevétka	क्रेवेयतका
Cheese	Сы́р	Sýr	सीर
Duck	У́тка	Útka	उतका
Butter	Ма́сло	Máslo	मासला
Sugar	Са́хар	Sákhar	साखर

Turkey	Инде́йка	Indéjka	इनजेयिका
Soap Powder	Стира́льный Порошо́к	Stirál'nyj Poroshók	स्तीरालनी पराशोक
Lobster	Ома́р	Omár	अमार
Broom	Шва́бра	Shvábra	शवाब्रा
Trash	Му́сор	Músor	मूसर

At the Department Store

Counter	Прила́вок	Prilávok	प्रिलावक
Thimbles	Напе́рстки	Napérstki	ना पेरस्तकी
Zippers	Застёжки "Мо́лния"	Zastjozhki "Mólnija"	जसतेजकी, "मोलनिया"
Buttons	Пу́говицы	Púgovitsy	पूगावित्सी
Buckles	Пря́жки	Prjázhki	प्रयाजकी
Thread	Ни́тка	Nítka	नितका
Lipsticks	Пома́да	Pomáda	पमादा
Talcum Powder	Та́льк	Tál'k	ताल्क
Razors	Бри́твы	Brítvy	ब्रित्वी
Face Cream	Кре́м Для́ Ли́ца	Krém Dljá Lítsa	क्रेम दल्या लित्सा
Scarves	Ша́рфы	Shárfy	शारफी

Gloves	Перча́тки	Perchátki	पिरछातकी
Belts	Ремни́	Remní	रेमनी
Hand Bags	Су́мочки	Súmochki	सूमचकी
Wallets	Бума́жники	Bumázhniki	बूमाजनीकी
Bracelets	Брасле́ты	Brasléty	ब्रसलियेती
Necklace	Ожере́лье	Ozherél'e	अजेरेलय
Pins	Бро́шки	Bróshki	ब्रोशकी
Ring	Кольцо́	Kol'tsó	कलत्सो
Electric Drill	Электри́ческая Дре́ль	Jelektrícheskaja Drél'	एलीकत्रिछसकया द्रैल
Curtain Rod	Карни́з	Karníz	कारनीज
Glue	Кле́й	Kléj	क्ले
Tiles	Ка́фель	Káfel'	कफेल
Paint	Кра́ска	Kráska	क्रासका
Elevator	Ли́фт	Líft	लिफ्त

Clothes

Shirt	Руба́шка	Rubáshka	रूबाशका
Trousers	Брю́ки	Brjúki	ब्रयूकी
Slip	Комбина́ция	Kombinátsija	कमबीनात्सया
Dress	Пла́тье	Plát'e	पलाचेय
Skirt	Ю́бка	Júbka	यूबका
Tights	Колго́ты	Kolgóty	कलगोति
Jacket	Жаке́т	Zhakét	जाकेट
Undershirt	Ма́йка	Májka	मायका
Underpants	Трусы́	Trusý	त्रूसी
Slippers	Та́пки	Tápki	तापकी
Socks	Носки́	Noskí	नसकी
Coat	Пальто́	Pal'tó	पलतो
Sweater	Сви́тер	Svíter	स्वीचेर
Sandals	Санда́лии	Sandálii	सनदाली
Shoes	Ту́фли	Túfli	तूफली
Mittens	Рукави́цы	Rukavítsy	रूकावितसी
Scarf	Ша́рф	Shárf	शर्फ
Boots	Сапоги́	Sapogí	सपागी
Hat	Ша́пка	Shápka	शापका
Nightgown	Ночна́я Руба́шка	Nochnája Rubáshka	नछनाया रूबाशका
Blouse	Блу́за	Blúza	ब्लूजा
Cap	Ке́пка	Képka	केपका
Tie	Га́лстук	Gálstuk	गालस्तूक
Shorts	Шо́рты	Shórty	शोरती
Tapemeasure	Сантиметро́вая Ле́нта	Santimetróvaja Lénta	सनचीमितरोवया लियन्ता
Shoe Lace	Шнуро́к	Shnurók	शनुरोक

In the Morning at Home

Pillow	Поду́шка	Podúshka	पदूषका
Curtain	Занаве́ска	Zanavéska	ज़नावयस्का
Sun	Со́лнце	Sólntse	सोनत्से
Window	Окно́	Oknó	अकनो
Bed	Крова́ть	Krovát’	क्रवाच
Blanket	Шерстяно́е Одея́ло	Sherstjanóe Odejálo	शिंसित्तचयाने अजीयाला
Pajamas	Пижа́ма	Pizháma	पिजामा
Undershirt	Ни́жняя Руба́шка	Nízhnjaja Rubáshka	निजनया रूबाशका
Hairbrush	Щётка Для́ Воло́с	Shhjotka Dljá Volós	शोयत्का दल्या वलोस
Mirror	Зе́ркало	Zérkalo	ज़ेयरकला
Spoon	Ло́жка	Lózhka	लोजका
Knife	Но́ж	Nózh	नोश
Napkin	Салфе́тка	Salfétka	सलफेयतका
Plate	Таре́лка	Tarélka	तारयलका
Fork	Ви́лка	Vílka	वीलका
Juice	Со́к	Sók	सोक
Toast	Грено́к	Grenók	ग्रेनोक
Tray	Подно́с	Podnós	पदनोस
Coffeepot	Кофейник	Koféjnik	काफेनिक
Cream	Сли́вки	Slívki	स्लीवकी
Dish Sponge	Тря́пка Для́ Мытья́ Посу́ды	Trjápka Dljá Myt’já Posúdy	तरयापका दल्या मितचिया पसूदी
Dish Towel	Ку́хонное Полоте́нец	Kúkhonnoe Poloténets	कूखनेये पलाचैनत्स

Buildings

Cottage	Котте́дж	Kottédzh	कातैज
Palace	Дворе́ц	Dvoréts	द्ववरेत्स
Lighthouse	Мая́к	Maják	मयाक
Library	Библиоте́ка	Bibliotéka	बिबलियाचेका
Church	Це́рковь	Tsérkov'	त्सेरकव
Temple	Хра́м	Khrám	ख्राम
Mosque	Мече́ть	Mechét'	मिचेच
Town Hall	Ра́туша	Rátusha	रतुशा
Castle	За́мок	Zámok	ज़ामक
Bank	Ба́нк	Bánk	बांक
Gallery	Галере́я	Galeréja	गलेरिया
Zoo	Зоопа́рк	Zoopárk	जापार्क
Café	Кафе́	Kafé	काफे
Club	Клу́б	Klúb	क्लूब
College	Ко́лледж	Kólledzh	कालेज
Museum	Музе́й	Muzéj	मूज़ेई
Hotel	Гости́ница	Gostínitsa	गसचीनित्सा
Office	О́фис	Ófis	ओफिस
Restaurant	Рестора́н	Restorán	रेस्तांरान
Supermarket	Суперма́ркет	Supermárket	सुपेरमार्केत
Theatre	Теа́тр	Téatr	चियातर
University	Университе́т	Universitét	
Circus	Ци́рк	Tsírk	त्सीक

Furniture

Plates	Таре́лки	Tarélki	तारयलकी
Mug	Кру́жка	Krúzhka	क्रूजका
Cupboard	Буфе́т	Bufét	बूफयेत

Picture	Карти́на	Kartína	करचीना
Vase	Ва́за	Váza	वाज़ा
Corner Cupboard	Углово́й Шка́ф	Uglovój Shkáf	उगलावोई श्क्फ
Cushion	Дива́нная Поду́шка	Divánnaja Podúshka	दीवानया पदूषका
Armchair	Кре́сло	Kréslo	क्रेसला
Chair	Сту́л	Stúl	स्तूल
Television	Телеви́зор	Televízor	चलेविजर
Desk	Па́рта	Párta	पारता
Wastepaper Basket	Корзи́на Для́ Бума́ги	Korzína Dljá Bumági	करजीना दल्या बूमागी
Table	Сто́л	Stól	सतोल
Lamp	Ла́мпа	Lámpa	लामपा
High Chair	Высо́кий Сту́л	Vysókij Stúl	विसोकी स्तूल
Chest Of Drawers	Комо́д	Komód	कामोद
Wardrobe	Гардеро́б	Garderób	गरदेरोब
Dressing Table	Туале́тный Сто́лик С Зе́ркалом	Tualétnyj Stólik S Zérkalom	तूवालयतनी सतोलीक स जेरकलम
Bed	Крова́ть	Krovát’	क्रवाच
Linen chest	Я́щик Для́ Белья́	Jáshhik Dljá Bel’já	याशिक दल्या बिलया
Tape Recorder	Магнитофо́н	Magnitofón	मगनिताफोन
Bookshelves	Кни́жные По́лки	Knízhnye Pólki	क्नीजनी पोलकी
Radio	Ра́дио	Rádio	राज्यो
Couch	Куше́тка	Kushétka	कुषेतका

In the Bathroom

Sponge	Гу́бка	Gúbka	गूबका
Soap	Мы́ло	Mýlo	मीला
Soap Dish	Мы́льница	Mýl'nitsa	मिलनित्सा
Warm Water	Тёплая Вода́	Tjoplaja Vodá	त्योपलया वदा
Bathtub	Ва́нна	Vánna	वाना
Backbrush	Щётка Для́ Мытья́ Спины́	Shhjotka Dljá Myt'já Spiný	शियोतका दल्या मिचिया स्पीनी
Medicine Cabinet	Апте́чка	Aptéchka	अपचेका
Bath Mat	Ко́врик Во́зле Ва́нны	Kóvrik Vózle Vánny	कोवरीक वोजल वानी
Toothbrush	Зубна́я Щётка	Zubnája Shhjotka	ज़ूबनाया शयोतका
Toothpaste	Зубна́я Па́ста	Zubnája Pásta	ज़ूबनाया पासता
Bandage	Би́нт	Bínt	बीन्त
Cotton	Ва́та	Váta	वाता
Towel Rack	Ве́шалка Для́ Полоте́нца	Véshalka Dljá Poloténtsa	विशालका दल्या पलाचेयनत्से
Towel	Полоте́нце	Poloténtse	पलाचेयनत्से
Bathrobe	Ба́нный Хала́т	Bánnyj Khalát	बाननी खलात
Shower	Ду́ш	Dúsh	दूष
Showercap	Ша́почка Для́ Душа́	Shápochka Dljá Dushá	शापचका दल्या दूषा

Shapes

Circle	Кру́г	Krúg	क्रुग
Square	Квадра́т	Kvadrát	कवादरात

Oval	Ова́л	Ovál	ओवल
Triangle	Треуго́льник	Treugól'nik	त्रेउगोनिक
Cone	Ко́нус	Kónus	कोनूस
Cube	Ку́б	Kúb	कूब
Arc	А́рка	Árka	आरका
Straight	Прямо́й	Prjamój	प्रिमोई

Animals

Cow	Коро́ва	Koróva	कारोवा
Horse	Ло́шадь	Lóshad'	लोशज
Bee	Пчела́	Pchelá	प्छीला
Lion	Ле́в	Lév	ल्येफ
Crow	Воро́на	Voróna	वरोना
Cat	Ко́шка	Kóshka	कोशका
Hen	Ку́рица	Kúritsa	कुरित्सा
Cuckoo	Куку́шка	Kukúshka	कुकुशा
Donkey	Осёл	Osjol	असयोल
Duck	У́тка	Útka	उतका
Dog	Соба́ка	Sobáka	सबाका
Frog	Лягу́шка	Ljagúshka	लिगूशका
Snake	Змея́	Zmejá	ज्मिया
Mouse	Мы́шь	Mýsh'	मिश
Pig	Свинья́	Svin'já	स्वीनणया
Owl	Сова́	Sová	सवा

Measuring

Scale	Весы́	Vesý	वेसी
Kitchen Scale	Ку́хонные Весы́	Kúhonnye Vesý	कुखनीय वेसी
Thermometer	Гра́дусник	Grádusnik	ग्रादुसनिक

Barometer	Баро́метр	Barómetr	बारोमेतर
Clock	Часы́	Chasý	छिसी
Calendar	Календа́рь	Kalendár’	कलेन्दार
Days	Дни́	Dní	द्नी
Months	Ме́сяц	Mésjats	मेस्यत्स
Weeks	Неде́ли	Nedéli	निजेली
Weather Wane	Флю́гер	Fljúger	फ्लूगेर
Measuring Cup	Ме́рная Ча́шка	Mérnaja Cháshka	मेरनया चाशका
Trailer Trackscale	Весы́ Для́ Грузовы́х Автомоби́лей	Vesý Dljá Gruzovýkh Avtomobílej	वेसी दल्या ग्रुज़ाविक अफतामाबिल्या
Ruler	Лине́йка	Linéjka	लिनयेका
Width	Ширина́	Shiriná	शीरीना
Height	Высота́	Vysotá	विसता

Movements

Stand	Стоя́ть	Stoját’	स्तयाच
Sit	Сиде́ть	Sidét’	सिजेयच
Lie Down	Лежа́ть	Lezhát’	लिजाच
Bend Over	Наклоня́ться	Naklonját’sja	नकलानियातस्या
Stretch	Потя́гиваться	Potjágivat’sja	पचयागीवत्स्या
Hop	Подпры́гивать	Podprýgivat’	पदवरीगीवच
Skip	Подска́кивать	Podskákivat’	पदस्काकीवच
Jump	Пры́гать	Prýgat’	परीगच
Look Around	Огля́дываться	Ogljádyvat’sja	अगलयादीवत्स्या
Walk	Ходи́ть	Khodít’	खाजीच
Run	Бе́гать	Bégat’	बियगच
Leap	Подпры́гнуть	Podprýgnut’	पदप्रीगनूच

Kneel	Стоя́ть На Коле́нях	Stoját' Na Kolénjakh	स्तयाच ना कालेनाख
Crouch	Приседа́ть	Prisedát'	प्रिसयेदाच
Throw	Броса́ть	Brosát'	ब्रसाच
Catch	Пойма́ть	Pojmát'	पईमाच
Climb	Взбира́ться	Vzbirát'sja	व्जबीरातस्या
Fall	Па́дать	Pádat'	पादच
Swing	Кача́ться	Kachát'sja	कछातस्या
Crawl	Ползти́	Polztí	पलजची
Vault	Вскочи́ть	Vskochít'	व्स्काछीच
Kick	Ударя́ть Ного́й	Udarját' Nogój	उदारयाच नागोय
Hit	Ударя́ть	Udarját'	उदारायाच
Pull	Тащи́ть	Tashhít'	ताशीच
Dive	Ныря́ть	Nyrját'	निरयाच
Swim	Пла́вать	Plávat'	पलावच
Skate	Ката́ться На Конька́х	Katát'sja Na Kon'kákh	कतातस्या ना कनकाख
Dance	Танцева́ть	Tantsevát'	तनसेवाच
Twirl	Кружи́ться	Kruzhít'sja	क्रुजित्स्या
Float	Пла́вать	Plávat'	पलावच

Usefulthings

Thumbtack	Кно́пка	Knópka	कनोपका
Safetypin	Англи́йская Була́вка	Anglíjskaja Bulávka	आगलिसकया बूलावका
Tape	Тесьма́	Tes'má	चेयसमा
Key	Клю́ч	Kljúch	कल्यूछ
Pin	Була́вка	Bulávka	बूलावका

Penknife	Перочи́нный Но́ж	Perochínnyj Nózh	पेयरछीननी नोश
Stamp	Ма́рка	Márka	मारका
String	Верёвка	Verjovka	विरयोवका
Ticket	Биле́т	Bilét	बिल्यत
Paper Clip	Скре́пка	Skrépka	स्क्रीपका
Thimble	Напе́рсток	Napérstok	नापेरस्तक
Hammer	Молото́к	Molotók	मलातोक
Nails	Гво́зди	Gvózdi	गवज़्दी
Featherduster	Перо́ Для́ Стира́ния Пы́ли	Peró Dljá Stiránija Pýli	पिरो दल्या सतिरानिया पीली
Scrubbrush	Полова́я Щётка	Polovája Shhjotka	पलावाया शयोतका
Mop	Шва́бра	Shvábra	शवाब्रा
Broom	Ве́ник	Vénik	वेनिक
Bucket	Ведро́	Vedró	विद्रा
Dustpan	Сово́к Для́ Му́сора	Sovók Dljá Músora	सवोक दल्या मूसरा
Electrical Outlet	Электрически Вы́ход	Jelektricheski Výkhod	एलीकत्रीछसकी विखद
Plug	Ште́псель	Shtépsel'	शतेपसेल
Cord	Шну́р	Shnúr	श्नूर
Vacuum Cleaner	Пылесо́с	Pylesós	पिलेसोस
Sewing Machine	Шве́йная Маши́на	Shvéjnaja Mashína	शवेनया मशीना
Tablecloth	Ска́терть	Skátert'	सकाचेयरच
Tub	Лоха́нь	Lokhán'	लखान
Ironing Board	Глади́льная Доска́	Gladíl'naja Doská	गलाजीलनया दसका

Iron	Утю́г	Utjúg	उचयूग
Clothes Line	Бельева́я Верёвка	Bel’evája Verjovka	बेलवाया विरयोवका
Clothespins	Прище́пки	Prishhépki	प्रिशेपकी
Laundry Basket	Бельева́я Корзи́на	Bel’evája Korzína	बेलेवाया करज़ीना
Needle	Иго́лка	Igólka	इगोलका

House, Aparment, Room, Furniture, Household Utensils

Block Of Flats	До́м	Dóm	दोम
Flat, Apartment	Кварти́ра	Kvartíra	कव्रचीरा
Balcony	Балко́н	Balkón	बलकोन
Hall	Коридо́р	Koridór	करीदोर
Study	Кабине́т	Kabinét	कबीनियत
Lavatory, Toilet	Туале́т	Tualét	तवालियत
Bathroom	Ва́нная	Vánnaja	वानया
Kitchen	Ку́хня	Kúkhnja	कूखन्या
Dining-Room	Столо́вая	Stolóvaja	स्तलोवया
Bedroom	Спа́льня	Spál’nja	स्पालनया
Ceiling	Потоло́к	Potolók	पतालोक
Floor	По́л	Pól	पोल
Wall	Стена́	Stená	स्तीना
Window	Окно́	Oknó	अकनो
Door	Две́рь *F.*	Dvér’	द्वैर
Chair	Сту́л	Stúl	स्तूल
Desk, Table	Сто́л	Stól	स्तौल

Armchair	Кре́сло	Kréslo	क्रैसला
Shelf	По́лка	Pólka	पोलका
Lamp	Ла́мпа	Lámpa	लाम्पा
Settee	Дива́н	Diván	जीवान
Telephone	Телефо́н	Telefón	चेलेफोन
Quilt	Одея́ло	Odejálo	अजेयाला
Bed Sheet	Простыня́	Prostynjá	प्रस्तीनया
Pillow	Поду́шка	Podúshka	पदूषका
Pillowcase	На́волочка	Návolochka	नावलछका
Carpet, Rug	Ковёр	Kovjor	कवयोर
Night Table	Ту́мбочка	Túmbochka	तुमबचका

Russianverbs

Бра́ть	To Take
Бри́ть	To Shave
Броса́ть	To Throw
Вари́ть	To Boil
Ве́шать	To Hang
Ви́деть	To See
Включа́ть	To Switch On
Возвраща́ть	To Return Smth. To Smbdy.
Возвраща́ться	To Comeback
Вспомина́ть	To Recall
Встреча́ть	To Meet

Выступа́ть-	To Perform
Входи́ть	To Enter
Выбира́ть	To Choose
Выходи́ть	To Exit
Говори́ть	To Talk
Дава́ть	To Give
Подари́ть	To Gift
Де́лать	To Do
Ду́мать	To Think
Жела́ть	To Wish
Забыва́ть	To Forget
За́втракать	To Have Breakfast
Замеча́ть	To Notice
Запомина́ть	To Remember
Позвони́ть	To Ring Up
Игра́ть	To Play
Изуча́ть	To Learn
Иска́ть	To Search
Кра́сить	To Paint
Крича́ть	To Shout
Ку́шать	To Eat
Ложи́ться	To Lie Down
Меша́ть	To Disturb
Мо́чь	To Be Able To

Начина́ть	To Start
Обе́дать	To Have Lunch
Обеща́ть	To Promise
Одева́ть	To Dress Up Smbdy.
Одева́ться	To Dress Up Oneself
Опа́здывать	To Get Late
Отвеча́ть	To Answer
Ошиба́ться	To Be Mistaken
Па́дать	To Fall
Переводи́ть	To Translate
Пе́ть	To Sing
Писа́ть	To Write
Пи́ть	To Drink
Пла́кать	To Cry
Плати́ть	To Pay
Повторя́ть	To Repeat
Пока́зывать	To Show
Покупа́ть	To Buy
Понима́ть	To Understand
Приглаша́ть	To Invite
Продолжа́ть	To Continue
Разбива́ть	To Break
Разреша́ть	To Permit
Расска́зывать	To Narrate

Реша́ть	To Decide, To Solve
Слу́шать	To Hear
Слы́шать	To Listen
Смотре́ть	To Watch
Собира́ть	To Collect
Сообща́ть	To Inform
Спра́шивать	To Ask
Стро́ить	To Build
Тра́тить	To Spend
Тро́гать	To Touch
У́жинать	To Have Dinner
Умира́ть	To Die
Учи́ть	To Study, To Teach

II

Glossary

Адрес	Address
Актриса	Actress
Американец	American
Английский	English
Англичанин	English Man
Анкета	Form
Апельсин	Orange
Апрель	April
Аудитория	Auditorium
Бабушка	Grandmother
Банк	Bank
Бар	Bar
Батон	Long Loaf
Без	Without
Бензин	Petrol, Gasoline
Беречь	To Keep, To Spare
Беречься	To Be Beware
Бить	To Beat
Болеть	To Be Ill
Больница	Hospital
Большой	Large, Big
Брат	Brother
Брать	To Take
Брюки	Trousers

Булка	Bun, Loaf
Булочка	Roll
Бывать	To Frequent
Быстрый	Fast, Quick
Быть	To Be, Will,Shall
Ведь	As
Великобритания	Great Britain
Весь	All
Вечер	Evening, Party
Вид	Type, Form
Видеть	To See
Вода	Water
Возраст	Age
Вокзал	Railway Station
Вон	Over There
Вопрос	Question
Вот	Here, There
Врач	Doctor
Время	Time
Всегда	Always
Встречаться	To Meet
Вторник	Tuesday
Входить	To Enter
Вчера	Yesterday
Выбор	Choice
Выборы	Elections
Выиграть	To Win
Высший	Superior, Highest
Выходить	To Exit
Германия	Germany

Герой	Hero
Глаз	Eye
Говорить	To Speak, To Talk
Год	Year
Гордость	Pride
Город	City
Гость	Guest
Давать	To Give
Даже	Even
Далеко	Far
Двадцать	Twenty
Дверь	Door
Дедушка	Grandfather
Декабрь	December
Делать	To Do
Дело	Work
День	Day
Деревня	Village
Дерево	Tree
Дети	Children
Детский	Children's
Детство	Childhood
До	Till, Up To
Добрый	Kind, Good
Долго	Long
Должен	Must
Дом	House
Дома	At Home
Домохозяйка	Housewife
Дорогой	Dear, Expensive,Valuable,Darling

Друг	Friend
Дыня	Melon
Дядя	Uncle
Европа	Europe
Его	His
Её	Her
Есть	To Have,Is
Ещё	Still,Yet, More, Even
Жаль	To Feel Sorry (For)
Жар	Heat
Же	Indeed, After All
Желать	To Wish
Железо	Iron
Жена	Wife
Женатый	Married
Живой	Living, Alive
Жидкость	Liquid, Fluid
Жить	To Live
Журнал	Magazine
Завтра	Tomorrow
За	For; Behind;Beyond
Завод	Factory
Задание	Task
Заказывать	To Order, To Book
Зал	Hall
Замок	Castle
Замок	Lock
Замужем	Married(Said Of Women Only)
Заниматься	To Be Occupied,Engaged
Заполнять	To Fill, Complete

Засмеяться	To Begin To Laugh
Звонить	To Call, Ring
Здание	Building
Здесь	Here, At This Point
Земля	Earth, Ground
Зимой	In Winter
Знамя	Banner
Знать	To Know
Играть.	To Play
Идти	To Go, To Come, To Move On Foot
Из	From
Имя	Name
Индиец	Indian
Индия	India
Инженер	Engineer
Институт	Institute
Интересно	Interestingly
Испания	Spain
Испанский	Indian
Италия	Italy
Итальянский	Italian
Июль	July
Июнь	June
К	To; Зу; On; Towards
Как	How
Какой	Which
Каникулы	Vacation
Карандаш	Pencil
Кастрюля	Saucepan
Кафе	Cafe, Coffee Shop

Китай	China
Китайский	Chinese
Клуб Club	
Книга	Book
Коммерсант	Businessman
Комната	Room
Конверт	Envelope
Конкретно	Specifically
Конфета	Candy
Корень	Root
Кот	Tomcat
Который	Which, Who,That
Красивый	Beautiful,Handsome
Кровь	Blood
Круглый	Round
Кто	Who
Купить	To Buy
Ложка	Spoon
Легко	Easily
Лекция	Lecture
Лет	Years
Летний	Summery
Летом	In Summer
Лётчик	Pilot
Ли	Whether
Ложиться	To Lay
Лук	Onion
Луч	Ray
Люк	Manhole
Магазин	Shop
Мальчик	Boy

Мама	Mummy
Матч	Match
Мебель	Furniture
Медь	Copper
Метро	Metro
Младший	Younger
Много	Many, Much, Lot
Можно	One Can, May
Молодёжь	Youth, Young People
Молодой	Young
Молодость	Youth
Море Sea	
Мочь	Can, May
Муж	Husband
Мужчина	Man,Male
Музей	Museum
Мышь	Mouse
Над	Above
Надо	Have To
Налево	On The Left
Например	For Example
Напротив	Opposite
Начинать	To Start, To Begin
Не	Not
Недалеко	Not Far
Неделя	Week
Немецкий	German
Нести	To Carry
Нестись	To Rush Along, Zip Along
Ни	Neither
Но	But

Новость	News
Новый	New
Нож	Knife
Ножницы	Scissors
Номер	Number
Нормально	Fine,Normal
Нос	Nose
Ночной	Overnight, Nocturnal
Ночь	Night
Ноябрь	November
Нужно	Must
Оба	Both
Обожать	To Love,Adore
Огромный	Huge, Enormous, Vast
Одежда	Clothes
Однажды	Once,One Day
Окно	Window
Около	About, Around,Near
Октябрь	October
Опаздывать	To Be Late
Орех	Nut
Останавливаться	To Come To A Stop
Ответ	Answer, Reply
Отдыхать	To Rest, Relax
Отец	Father
Отправляться	Set Off, Depart
Отставать	Lag Behind
Отсюда	From Here
Очень	Very, Much,Greatly
Очки	Spectacles
Ошибка	Mistake

Ошибаться	To Be Wrong
Папа	Papa
Пар	Steam, Vapour
Пение	Singing
Пенсия	Pension
Переводчик	Translator,Interpreter
Переговоры	Talks ,Negotiations
Петь	To Sing
Писатель	Writer, Author
Письмо	Letter
Пить	To Drink
Пламя	Flame
Планетарий	Planetarium
Плащ	Raincoat
Племя	Tribe
Плохо	Poorly,Ill
Площадь	Area
Победа	Victory, Win
Подруга	Female Friend
Подумать	Think For A While
Познакомиться	To Get Acquainted
Пока	While,Till,Meanwhile
Поле	Field
Половина	Half
Польский	Polish
Польша	Poland
Помогать	To Help
Портфель	Briefcase
Посереди́не	In The Middle
После	After, Since
Потом	Then, Later

Почта	Post Office
Почти	Almost
Просьба	Request
Правильно	Correctly, Rightly
Предлагать	To Propose,Offer, Suggest
Приблизительно	Nearly, About, Approximately
Привет	Hi
Примерно	Approximately
Приятно	Nicely,Pleasantly
Приятный	Pleasant, Nice
Проверить	To Inspect, To Check
Проводить	To Spend Time
Просить	To Request
Простить	Forgive, Pardon
Прошлый	Past,Last
Прямо	Straight,Direct
Птица	Bird
Пятница	Friday
Работать	To Work
Рад	Glad
Развод	Divorce
Разговаривать	To Converse
Разрешить	To Permit
Рано	Early
Рассказчик	Narrator, Storyteller
Ресторан	Restaurant
Рисовать	To Draw, Paint
Ровно	Exactly
Родители	Parents
Родиться	To Be Born

Рожь	Rye
Россия	Russia
Русский	Russian
Ручка	Pen
Рядом	Alongside,Near
Самовар	Samovar
Сахар	Sugar
Свежий	Fresh
Сделать	To Do
Сдача	Change
Сегодня	Today
Сейчас	Just Now, Presently
Семья	Family
Семя	Seed
Сентябрь	September
Сестра	Sister
Сказать	To Say
Сколько	How Much, How Many
Скорость	Speed
Слева	To The Left
Слишком	Too Much
Словарь	Dictionary
Слушать	To Listen
Смеяться	To Laugh
Смотреть	To Look, Watch
Советовать	To Advise
Спасать	To Save, Rescue
Спасибо	Thank You
Спастись	To Escape
Спешить	To Hurry, Hasten

Сплошь	Everywhere,Entirely
Спокойный	Calm
Справа	To The Right
Стоит	To Cost
Ставить	To Put, To Place
Стакан	Glass
Стихи	Poetry
Стол	Table
Стоять	To Stand
Студент	Student
Студентка	Student (F)
Стул	Chair
Сумка	Bag
Сутки	Day
Сухой	Dry
Сходство	Resemblance
Счастливый	Happy; Lucky; Fortunate
Счёт	Score
Считать	To Count, To Consider
США	USA
Сын	Son
Также	Also, As Well,Too
Такие	Such
Там	There
Твой	Yours
Театр	Theatre
Телевизор	Television
Теперь	Now, At Present
Тетрадь	Notebook
Тогда	Then, At That Time

Только	Only, Just
Торопиться	To Hurry, Hasten
Тот	That
Точное	Exact, Precise, Accurate
Трудно	With Difficulty
Тут	Here
У-With,By,At	
Увлекаться	To Be Keen,To Take A Great Interest
Удобный	Comfortable, Convenient
Уже	Already
Улица	Street, Road
Урок	Class
Услышать	To Hear
Утро	Morning
Утром	In The Morning
Уходить	Leave,Go,Retire,Resign
Учиться	To Study (At), To Learn
Учитель	Teacher
Учительница	Teacher F.
Учить	To Teach, To Learn
Фамилия	Surname,Last Name
Февраль	February
Фильм	Movie
Фотография	Photograph
Франция	France
Французский	French
Футбол	Football
Хватать	To Suffice
Хинди	Hindi
Хлеб	Bread

Хороший	Good, Nice
Хотеть	To Want
Циркуль	Compasses
Чай	Tea
Часто	Often
Чей	Whose
Чем	Than
Чем-нибудь	Anything
Через	Through
Четверг	Thursday
Читать	To Read
Что	What
Шар	Ball, Sphere
Школа	School
Экзамен	Examination
Этаж	Floor
Это	This,It
Юноша	Youth
Январь	January
Япония	Japan
Японский	Japanese